THE
Crafter's
PATTERN
SOURCEBOOK

1,001 CLASSIC MOTIFS FROM AROUND
THE WORLD AND THROUGH THE AGES

MARY MacCARTHY

Trafalgar Square Publishing

For Jeremy

I would also like to thank Alison Wormleighton, Kate Haxell (for getting me started), Andy Vargo and the Librarians of the Norwich School of Art and Design.

First published in the United States of America in 1999 by
Trafalgar Square Publishing, North Pomfret, Vermont 05053

Printed in Hong Kong by Dai Nippon Printing Co.

First published in Great Britain in 1999
by Collins & Brown Limited

9 8 7 6 5 4 3 2 1

ISBN 1-57076-141-8

Library of Congress Catalog Card Number: 98-86211

Editor: Alison Wormleighton
Designer: Alison Lee
Illustrator: Kate Simunek
Computer artwork: Dominic Harris
Photographer: Matthew Dickens

Reproduction by Grafiscan, Italy

The pictures on pages 13, 113 and 153 appear by kind permission of Christie's Images.

CONTENTS

INTRODUCTION

Patterns have always fascinated me. As a child I would study the repeat motifs on wallpapers and curtains, working out what linked up with what to make such a smooth, continuous design. I was also intrigued by the wonderfully intricate children's book illustrations by artists such as Walter Crane, Kate Greenaway and Arthur Rackham. Even then I took ideas from them: I particularly remember a simple green stool with a mouse painted on the seat and matching curtains decorated with sugar mice.

As my interest in pattern and design grew over the years, I found inspiration in antique textiles and decorative china. When painting, decorating and designing furniture, fabrics and walls for my own home and for friends and clients, I have always delighted in the research the work entailed. Whether I am walking miles around museums, pouring over old books in libraries or visiting ancient buildings, I find the process enormously rewarding. In everyday life, too, I am always on the lookout for good patterns to use in one way or another – watching films, reading magazines…or just staring at the walls, like I did as a child.

For years I have had a book like *The Crafter's Pattern Sourcebook* at the back of my mind, although it would have been only for my own personal use as a decorative artist – a manual from which I could pull out patterns at will. Now it has become a reality, for use by all decorative artists, from embroiderers to stencilers and potters, indeed anyone who makes, designs and decorates.

The patterns are grouped into nine chapters, each corresponding to a different part of the world. At first it seemed a daunting task to come up with a thousand and

For the tieback, see page 116

Never feel guilty about copying patterns – designers have 'borrowed' ideas and drawn inspiration from each other's work since time immemorial. For example, in the 1800s fashionable homes boasted Grecian or Pompeiian wall paintings, Roman motifs on china and plaster, and so-called Etruscan rooms, all inspired by the newly discovered ruins of the ancient cities Pompeii and Herculaneum. Similarly, the Art Deco style of many a New York skyscraper from the 1920s is based on an ancient Egyptian theme. The Victorian designer William Morris, who produced an enormous number of innovative designs for a wide variety of crafts, including embroidery, weaving, stained glass and typography, was himself heavily influenced by English and French art of the Middle Ages, Italian Renaissance weaves and Islamic and Persian textile designs.

It is particularly intriguing to find the same patterns repeating themselves around the world. Sometimes the strictures of the craft are responsible for similar patterns, such as the weaves of South America, North Africa and some places in the Far East, but the reasons for other instances are not so obvious. For example, I came across some Chinese carvings and some Viking carvings of about the same time, 500 AD, which, despite their being from opposite sides of the world, were almost identical.

I based the designs in this book on patterns I found in an enormous variety of places. Knowing a particular pattern's provenance (see pages 191–192, where all the sources are listed) will help you to appreciate it, and many are extremely interesting. But don't let it influence how you use the design – every one of the patterns could be used for a variety of crafts and purposes. They are infinitely versatile.

Often a pattern lends itself better to some projects than to others. The scale is one factor – a small pattern, for example, would probably look insignificant on a large wall, while it could appear strong and intricate on a cushion. The actual shape of the surface which you are decorating will obviously have a

For the box, see page 56

one patterns, but as I researched designs through the ages for each chapter, it began to feel very like a voyage of discovery. On any given day I might come across a fine drawing of crocuses painted 3,500 years ago on a Minoan pot, or a sophisticated abstract pattern on a Navajo blanket. In the end, the problem was not how to produce a thousand designs but how to decide what I should leave out of the book.

For the jug, see page 76

bearing, too. That is why, for example, a design originally used on a wooden butter container from Norway looks perfectly at home on an embroidered curtain tieback (see page 4) – the shape and proportions are similar.

The decorative technique you will be using is another factor affecting the suitability of a design. If you are stamping with a potato or sponge, for instance, the image will need to be simple, whereas a linocut or stencil can be as complicated as your skill in cutting allows. An intricate design such as a vine with climbing tendrils would be impractical in appliqué but would look delicately elegant in embroidery.

There is obviously not enough space in this book to provide detailed instructions covering all of the crafts for which these designs are suitable, but a brief guide to

For the beret, see page 175

some of the principal crafts is given on pages 7–11. Instructions for adapting the designs, including how to use the acetate grids, are on page 6. Treat the book like a pick-'n'-mix counter: select a design, find another to go with it, then choose a complementary border. (There is advice on combining motifs and creating borders on page 12.)

To inspire you, we have made up some of the patterns as particular items, which are shown at the beginning of each chapter. None of these ideas bears any relation to the original source – indeed, that is part of the fun of using designs from the book. For example, the Indian design appliquéd onto the beret above was originally worked in leather on a camel saddle. The motifs on the appliqué tablecloth and pottery bowl on page 35 are both from the same source, a Greek amphora.

These examples have been made in colors typical or evocative of the regions from which the designs came: bright, lively colors for South America; quiet, subdued hues for England; earthy tones for Africa; beautiful, rich blues for Mediterranean countries. Of course, you don't have to use these colors in your own projects. The patterns in this book are shown in their simplest forms and in black and white, allowing you the freedom to devise your own decorative ideas.

For the cushion, see page 55

When deciding on colors I like to have a few photocopies to experiment with. I then choose three different combinations of crayons or pastels, so I can color in the photocopies. I may start with the background, sometimes in the most natural tone, and at other times in the darkest for a more dramatic effect. If it is a leafy, organic design, I will color it in with a variety of greens, blues or rusts. The bright colors can be left till last, to finish off, at which point the design really comes to life.

Color is highly personal but, if you have trouble deciding, you can always choose the shades that match the colors the project will be near – a room scheme, garment or whatever. I tend to choose bright and unexpected color combinations, but they are not always to everyone's taste. To begin with, it is probably best to choose a simple pattern and not more than three colors. Simplicity, along with balance and good proportion, is often the key to good design.

What I find particularly thrilling about using motifs and patterns taken from other cultures is trying to imagine the lives of the people who originally devised the patterns, and to picture how they

For the chair, see page 14

actually used them. I love the romance and excitement surrounding the designs and I aim to keep that spirit alive in the work I do today.

Mary MacCarthy

THE TECHNIQUES

The patterns in this sourcebook can be used in a wide variety of crafts, including appliqué, freehand embroidery, freehand painting, découpage, stenciling and stamping. In addition, by utilizing the special grids supplied with the book, they can be used for needlepoint, cross stitch, Swiss darning (duplicate stitch) and knitting. This chapter includes instructions for adapting the patterns to your own requirements, and the basic techniques for the crafts that most often use this type of design. There is also advice on designing patterns by repeating one motif, combining two or more motifs, and creating borders.

USING AN ACETATE GRID

Needlepoint and cross stitch are worked from a chart based on a grid, with one square corresponding to one stitch. Multi-colored knitting and Swiss darning are also worked from grid-based charts, in which squares or, preferably, rectangles correspond to the stitches. To convert a design to one of these charts, decide on its overall dimensions in terms of stitches (for example, 30 stitches wide by 40 stitches high) and use an acetate grid with at least that many squares (or rectangles for knitting and Swiss darning) across each dimension. Enlarge or reduce the design to the size of the portion of the grid you are using, and tape the grid over it. Photocopy them together, enlarging or reducing to the desired finished size of the design. (If you don't have access to a photocopier, enlarge or reduce the design to the desired finished size using the grid method shown below right, then either draw a grid of the appropriate number of squares/rectangles onto it, or trace it onto transparent graph paper.) Finally, color in each square in the appropriate shade.

TRANSFERRING A DESIGN

To transfer a motif to paper, either trace it over a light source or photocopy it. A traced or photocopied motif can be transferred onto fabric in one of the following ways:

■ Place dressmaker's carbon paper face down between the right side of the fabric and the tracing/photocopy. Run a tracing wheel (or a pen for fine detail) over the outlines.

■ For a simple shape, draw around a template using a pencil, tailor's chalk, a fade-away pen (which fades gradually) or a water-soluble marker pen (which can be removed with water).

■ With light fabrics, lay the fabric face up over the tracing/photocopy on a lightbox (or against a window) and trace the outlines with a pencil, tailor's chalk, fade-away pen or water-soluble marker pen.

■ Retrace the design on the reverse of the tracing/photocopy using a transfer pencil, then iron it onto the fabric, reverse side down.

A traced or photocopied motif can be transferred onto an opaque hard surface, such as cardboard, pottery, wood or plaster, in either of the following ways:

■ Place graphite paper between the tracing/photocopy and the surface and draw over the outlines.

■ Using a soft pencil, scribble over the back of the tracing/photocopy, or just retrace the design onto the back. Now place the tracing, right side up, against the surface and draw over the outline using a hard pencil.

ENLARGING OR REDUCING A MOTIF

The simplest way to enlarge or reduce a design is on a photocopier. Pick a distinctive part of the motif and work out the size you want it to be on the finished design. Measure the same part on the page of the book. Divide the desired size by the actual size and multiply by 100 – this is the percentage you need to enlarge the motif by. For example, if you want a motif to be 4in (10cm) long and in this book it is 3in (7.5cm), enlarge it by 133 per cent.

If you don't have access to a photocopier, use a grid as shown below.

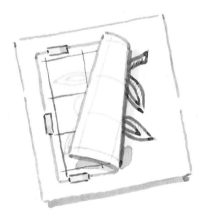

1 *On tracing paper that is the size of the original motif, draw a grid of 2in (5cm) squares. Lay it over the design and tape it in place around the edges with masking tape.*

2 *On a plain piece of paper that is the desired size, draw a grid with the same number of squares but proportionately larger or smaller. Copy the original lines onto the new grid, square by square.*

A BRIEF GUIDE TO THE CRAFTS

KNITTING

Colored motifs can be knitted into garments using charts that are included in patterns or that you design yourself. The design is converted to a box grid (see opposite) that corresponds to the number of stitches and rows and the shape of the relevant part of the garment. When designing on graph paper, allow for the fact that knit stitches — which the graph paper shows as square — are wider than they are tall, so you may need to elongate the design to compensate. (The acetate grid with rectangles allows for this.) Stocking (stockinette) stitch is the easiest to work with.

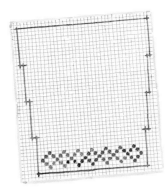

1 To add a motif to a sleeve, work out the number of stitches in the first row; mark off this number of squares near the bottom of the grid. Use the pattern tension measurement to work out the number of rows up to the armhole, then mark the top row on the paper. Mark off the sides, stepping them for any increases. Add the design.

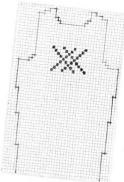

2 Follow the same procedure for any part of the garment where motifs will appear. For the front or back, mark off the armhole, shoulder and neck shaping, and any increases at the side seams. Use the completed chart in conjunction with the knitting pattern, reading the chart from left to right for a knit row and from right to left for a purl row.

SWISS DARNING (DUPLICATE STITCH)

With this, even non-knitters can add designs to garments knitted in stocking stitch. The design is embroidered in stitches that look like the knit stitches they cover.

A chart like a knitting color chart is used as a guide, either part of a colorwork knitting pattern or one you make (see above).

It is easiest to work Swiss darning before the garment is assembled. Use a tapestry needle and yarn of the same type and thickness as the yarn of the garment.

1 Start at the bottom right-hand corner of the design, securing the yarn at the back with a couple of stitches. Bring the needle up through the base of the first stitch, then take the needle from right to left under the base of the stitch above. Complete the stitch by inserting the needle into the base of the original stitch.

2 Working from right to left, use the same method to cover all the stitches of that particular color in the row. To embroider the row above, make stitches by inserting the needle from left to right, and work along the row from left to right. The next row is worked like the first row, and so on till all the rows in that color are finished. Repeat for the other colors.

NEEDLEPOINT

Needlepoint covers the canvas with stitches, usually in wool. A frame helps prevent it distorting. Use a tapestry needle and 1–4 strands of yarn, depending on the yarn. To transfer a design to canvas, mark the center lines on both, and tape or pin the canvas over the design, lining up the center marks. Draw the outlines with a waterproof marker, then, if desired, paint in the whole design with acrylic paints. For detailed work, a color chart showing each stitch is helpful; make one using the acetate grid in the book (see opposite).

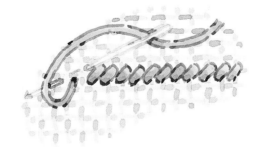

1 Many stitches are suitable but tent stitch is by far the most common, as it is very durable and reproduces detail well. Use the variation known as continental tent stitch when you are working a single line of stitches, whether horizontally, vertically or diagonally. The needle is taken diagonally under two canvas intersections.

2 Use the basketweave tent stitch variation for everything except single lines of stitches. It is worked either diagonally down the canvas with the needle taken vertically under two threads, or diagonally up the canvas with the needle taken horizontally under two threads. (At the end of a row it is inserted diagonally under two intersections.)

The Techniques

CROSS STITCH

This is worked over a particular number of threads, following a chart in which a square represents one stitch. (To convert a design to a chart, see page 6.) It is worked on fabric with an inherent grid, such as evenweave or gingham.

Widely used in folk art, cross stitch is the best-known type of counted thread embroidery. As well as detailed work like lettering and borders, it is suitable for filling in. It is often worked over two threads but can be over any number. The stitch size, embroidery thread or wool, and number of strands can all vary.

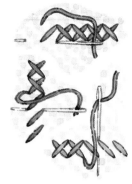

1 Use a tapestry needle, and hold the fabric taut in a hoop or on a frame. The diagonals should slant the same way. Each stitch can be completed before the next is begun (top diagram), or all the diagonals slanting one way can be worked and then all the diagonals slanting the other way (center and bottom diagrams).

2 To work cross stitch or other counted thread embroidery on fabric that doesn't have a visible grid, such as fine linen, tack (baste) a piece of evenweave fabric, or 'waste canvas', to the right side of the fabric. Embroider through both layers at once. Carefully pull away the waste canvas one thread at a time, leaving the embroidered design in place.

FREEHAND EMBROIDERY

This type of embroidery is worked independently of the background and so does not require a stitch chart. Innumerable stitches can be used, making virtually any design possible. Because precise counting of threads is not done, the designs tend to be freer and less geometric-looking than those involving counted-thread embroidery. A variety of fabrics may be used, but cotton and linen are the most common. The thread may be stranded or unstranded; thick or thin; matt or shiny; and cotton, wool or metallic.

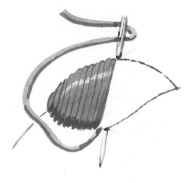

1 Transfer the design to the right side of the fabric using dressmaker's carbon paper, then place the fabric over the inner ring of a hoop; push the outer ring over it. Thread an embroidery needle, but do not knot the thread (the ends are woven in).

2 Use a variety of hand stitches to outline, such as running, chain, stem or back stitch; to fill in the design, stitches such as satin stitch (shown here) or long-and-short stitch; and, to add texture, stitches such as bullion knots or French knots.

MACHINE EMBROIDERY

Spectacular effects are possible with machine embroidery, even using just the simplest swing-needle sewing machine. Backing the fabric either permanently with interfacing or temporarily with tear-away stabilizer makes it easier to stitch on. Conventional sewing thread may be used, but machine-embroidery threads come in matt or luster finishes, with metallic and variegated-color versions too. Using a different thread on the top from the one on the bobbin creates interesting effects. Experiment first, then transfer a design to fabric and embroider it, using either simple or free machine embroidery, or both.

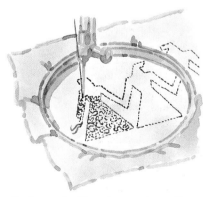

1 Even simple machine embroidery can look stunning. Use a normal presser foot (or an open-toe foot, for better visibility) and straight and zigzag stitch, in different stitch widths, lengths and tensions. For machine satin stitch, use a zigzag stitch with a very low stitch length. Also experiment with crosshatching and with zigzagging over a cord.

2 For free embroidery, lower or cover the teeth, and remove the foot (or use a darning foot to protect fingers). Lay the fabric right-side up on the outer rim of a hoop and push the inner rim into it so the fabric is taut. Set the stitch length and width to 0, then slowly stitch, guiding the hoop in different directions. Try out different tensions and stitch widths.

COUCHED BEADING

There are many ways to decorate fabric with beads, including sewing them on individually either as scattered highlights (a technique often used for decorating embroidery) or in groups forming repeat motifs. A faster method, known as couched beading, which is often used in Native American beadwork, is shown here. Choose a design in which the shapes are bold and simple. Both linear designs, such as a scroll shape, and filled-in shapes are possible. You will need to plan the color sequence and the number of beads of each color beforehand. The fabric must be stretched taut on a frame or in a hoop.

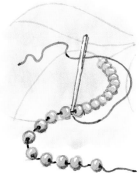

1 Thread a beading needle with strong thread, secure it on the wrong side of the fabric and bring it up at one end of the motif. Thread the correct number of beads onto it, and lay them along the marked outline. With a sewing needle and sewing thread, make tiny stitches between the beads to couch them in place, pulling the bead thread taut as you do so.

2 As you secure each bead, slide the next one up close to it. When you reach the end, fasten off both threads at the back. Repeat for the remaining lines of beads in the design. A filled-in motif looks more interesting if it has a linear element (such as the veins on a leaf) so that different colored lines of beads can be part of the design, but you have to plan the design carefully.

APPLIQUÉ

Appliqué involves applying cut-out fabric shapes to contrasting fabric to create a design. Motifs involving straight edges or gentle curves are best for beginners, while those with sharp points, deep 'valleys', intricate or deep curves, or small pieces are for the more experienced. Turned-edge hand appliqué, as shown here, is the traditional technique, but a faster method involves attaching the fabric pieces with fusible web then zigzag stitching over the raw edges; on felt or wool, straight-stitching can be used instead, since neither fabric will fray.

1 Make templates for the shapes to the desired finished size, and draw around each shape on the right side of the fabric, using a fade-away pen. Cut out with a ¼in (6mm) seam allowance all around. Tack (baste) the pieces in place at least ⅝in (1.5cm) in from the raw edges.

2 Snip off any outward corners and clip into any inward corners and curves within the seam allowances. Hand sew the pieces in place with slip-stitch (or blanket, feather, stab or cross stitch), using the needle to roll the seam allowance under as you work around the edge of each fabric piece.

DÉCOUPAGE

This craft involves gluing cut-out pieces of paper to a hard surface and then varnishing repeatedly until they look like hand-painted decoration. To use motifs from this book, choose shapes that are suitable for cutting out. The motifs from the Oriental chapter could be cut out from black paper and used with gloss varnish for a lacquerwork effect. Shapes cut out from plain paper can be decorated with paint or pencils (but do not use crayons or pastels, which could smudge) then sealed with diluted white household glue.

1 Photocopy the shapes onto plain-colored or patterned paper (or onto white paper which you then decorate with paints or pencils and seal with white household glue diluted one part glue to two parts water). Cut out the shapes.

2 Plan the arrangement then apply white household glue to the surface; stick the shapes in place, pressing out any air bubbles. When the glue is dry, apply at least three coats of acrylic or polyurethane varnish, allowing it to dry between coats.

The Techniques

CUTTING STENCILS

For stenciling, a design has to be broken down into separate shapes held together by 'ties' about ⅛in (3mm) wide and 3–4in (7.5–10cm) apart. Their precise size, shape and position depend on the design, since they need to be of a similar scale, to follow the lines of the motif and to be at natural points in the design. You can create separate stencils for each color, or use one stencil for all colors (see below). Be sure to cut on a cutting mat or thick cardboard. Stencils can be made from either oiled manila card or acetate. To draw on acetate, use a marker pen that will write on shiny surfaces.

1 Transfer the design to the card or acetate (see page 6), leaving a 2in (5cm) margin all around. Holding a sharp craft knife nearly upright, cut towards yourself from the center of the design outward. Hold the stencil with your other hand, keeping it out of the path of the knife.

2 Use a single stroke to cut curves, turning the stencil, not the knife. If desired, mark the center of each edge with cut-out notches or drawn lines to use for positioning when stenciling. If you accidentally cut through a tie, patch it with pieces of tape the width of the tie, on front and back.

STENCILING

Acrylic and stenciling paints work best, but emulsion (latex) can be used. Oil paints are tricky to apply and slow-drying. Fabric paints and acrylics are both suitable for stenciling onto fabric. Spray paint is an alternative, but is messy and so requires considerable masking; also, the fumes are hazardous.

Different textures can be produced by varying the brush action or using a sponge instead of a brush. Applying a slightly lighter color (or no color at all) in the center of a motif, or using a heavier brush action around the edge, creates an illusion of depth.

1 With low-tack masking tape, fasten the stencil to the surface and mask out any areas on the stencil that are not to be painted in the first color. Mix up all the paint you are likely to need, and put a little of it on the palette.

2 Take up a tiny amount of paint on a barely damp stencil brush; work it well into the brush using a circular motion on the palette. Stencil with circular movements (or back and forth on narrow areas), holding the brush upright.

CUTTING STAMPS

Stamps you cut yourself can be as basic as potatoes or as sophisticated as linocuts. Sponges are both easy and effective, providing a happy medium between the two. A kitchen sponge or a bath sponge will add texture to bold, simple shapes, while high-density upholstery foam and polystyrene are better for detailed or intricate motifs. Sticking the sponge to a wooden backing makes it easier to handle but is not essential (except for polystyrene, which should be stuck to a backing before the pattern is cut out).

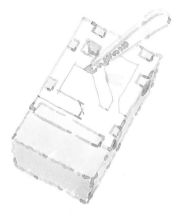

1 Place the sponge on a cutting mat and tape the tracing/photocopy on top. Using a sharp craft knife, cut around the design, through the tracing/photocopy at the same time.

2 Cut out a wooden backing to make the stamp easier to handle. Mount the stamp on the wood using contact adhesive or wood glue. You could also add a knob to the backing if desired.

STAMPING

Stamps can be used in combination as well as singly. For example, a stylish geometric border created from simple shapes could complement a more complicated motif perfectly. Overstamping – stamping one motif on top of another in a different color, once the first is dry – also opens up new possibilities.

Acrylic, emulsion (latex) and ceramic paints, and also ink, are all suitable, depending on the surface you are stamping. (To stamp on fabric, use a rubber stamp rather than sponge, as sponge is too soft.)

1 Plan the position of the image: by inverting or rotating the motif and/or grouping repeats together, you can create more complex patterns. Spread an even coating of a water-based paint such as emulsion on an old plate or roller tray.

2 Press the stamp evenly into the paint on the plate, without saturating it. Now press it evenly and firmly onto the surface being decorated, removing it carefully to avoid smudging. Reload the sponge with paint, and continue stamping.

FREEHAND PAINTING

With the designs in this book, freehand painting is within the capabilities of even the least artistic novice painter. For flat, stylized patterns, shading and highlighting are not necessary, though you can introduce a little to realistic motifs such as animals. Virtually any design can be used, and practically any surface can be decorated, provided the appropriate paint (fabric paints for fabric, ceramic paints for tiles, and so on) is used. A small amount of hand painting can be an attractive way of embellishing stenciled designs; you can even fill in the ties on stenciled images to make them look as though the entire design is hand-painted.

1 Very straight stripes can be painted by running low-tack masking tape along the edges. If you paint them freehand, running your little finger along a ruler placed parallel to the line helps prevent wobbles. A good way of painting spots is to wrap masking tape around the bristles of a stencil brush, 1/4 in (6mm) from the end, and twirl the brush round to apply the paint.

2 Stripes and/or spots can look good combined with more elaborate motifs. To make a conventional brush stroke for, say, a flower, start with the point of the brush on the surface you are decorating, then lightly press the brush down onto the surface and slightly drag it along, before finally lifting it off. For a more realistic, shaded effect, make the outer edges slightly darker and the center lighter.

PAINTING ON POTTERY AND PAPIER MÂCHÉ

Painting your own designs onto pottery before it is fired in a kiln is very easy and rewarding, and many of the designs in this book lend themselves to bowls and plates, cups and saucers, jugs and vases. The decoration is applied to the plain bisqueware or to a base color, using specialist underglaze colors. Papier mâché items are suitable for a similar style of decoration, using water-based paints. To ensure the dry papier mâché will come off the mold, cover the mold first with clingfilm (plastic wrap).

1 For bisqueware, transfer the design using graphite transfer paper, or draw it on with a pencil. Use artist's brushes and underglaze colors to paint the design, or you can stamp or stencil it with these paints. An underglaze pencil can be used to outline if desired. When the paint is dry, remove visible pencil/graphite lines with a rubber (eraser).

2 To make papier mâché by the layered method, cover a mold in 4–6 layers of newspaper strips dipped in diluted white household glue. Leave to dry, then remove the mold. Prime with emulsion (latex). When dry, transfer the design to the surface as for bisqueware. Apply color using a paintbrush. When dry, seal with acrylic or polyurethane varnish.

The Techniques

DESIGNING WITH MOTIFS

A motif is quite simply a form. It can be used on its own or repeated to create a pattern. The arrangement of the motifs is important – this is where the skill of pattern-making lies. Think of it as a game in which you take a motif, multiply it by photocopying or tracing, then play with the patterns in different ways.

Work out a grid and see how the duplicated motifs look when placed on each cross. Try reversing half of the motifs and alternating the two versions. Some designs can be turned upside down as well as reversed, increasing the scope even more. Take another motif and repeat it in a single row and you have a border. The possibilities are endless.

Find a design that appeals and will look well balanced and 'settled' on the object you are decorating. It is better to be bold in your choice than too delicate, although you obviously don't want to be heavy-handed with it.

For honeysuckle motif, see page 43 (no. 48)

A bold, strong motif can look smart on its own, as the honeysuckle design of the needlepoint cushion on page 36 demonstrates, while a single line or simple border will give it definition. Plant and animal motifs lend themselves well to being used in this way. The heart and oak design shown below could be embroidered in a scale that fills the space on a round cushion. Or a huge painted Chinese dragon could sprawl dramatically up the wall of a staircase. Though very different, both designs can be used on their own to great effect.

When combining different patterns for an all-over design – for example, on a stenciled wall – you could pick one dominant design and set it off with a small, quite simple motif, repeating the motifs alternately across the wall. With ample spacing, this can create an effective visual rhythm within the design.

For Elizabethan heart and oak design, see page 143 (no. 41)

Having a theme for several related projects can be fun, so consider combining motifs that have the same origin – for example, Native American designs. You could fill a room with a delightful combination of patterns, including perhaps a frieze, a painted lampshade, a cushion and a floor

For bouquet and flower motifs, see page 142 (no. 33, 34)

cloth. This is also a good way of ensuring that patterns have an affinity with each other and so look right together.

On the other hand, unlikely combinations can look very striking and fresh. Simple geometric shapes mix well with dynamic curvilinear designs. For example, a diamond could be combined with the Celtic double-headed eagle shown below, as painted decoration on a wooden chest.

For double-headed eagle motif, see page 137 (no. 2)

A rich background can be built up by using rows of four or five different patterns, with a simple border pattern running between each motif. Together they may create an exotic Indian or Provençal effect.

The border is, in fact, one of the most useful decorative devices, defining the basic shape of an object and at the same time unifying the design. A border can even be used as the only decorative feature. Edging an appliquéd tablecloth, or the cuffs of a knitted sweater, it will add style as well as definition, whether it is as simple as a single Celtic line or as rich as a William Morris leafy tapestry.

Start a border at the middle and work outwards. You can add an extra leaf or dot if necessary to fill any gaps at the corners. There are two ways to deal with the corners themselves: either create a mitre at each corner by masking it diagonally and working the design up to it, or take a small section of the design and set it on its own at each corner.

Whatever combinations of borders, repeated single motifs and central patterns you select, your creations will be your own. Remember, you are the ultimate judge of the success of your design.

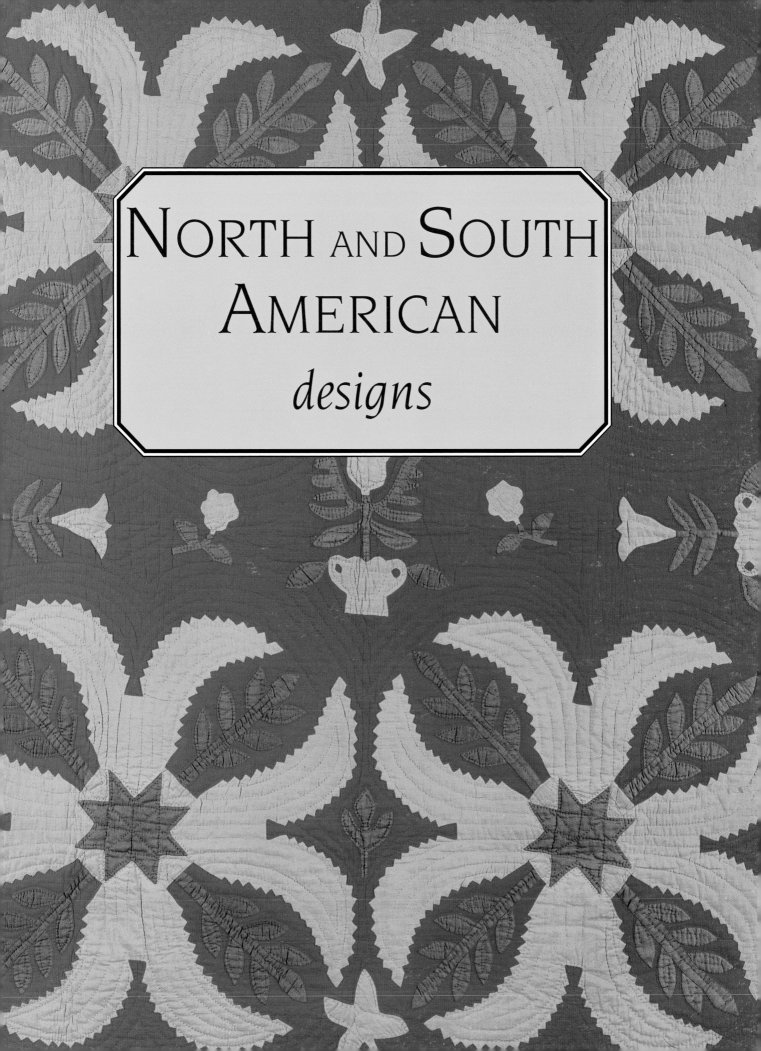

NORTH AND SOUTH AMERICAN

designs

NORTH AND SOUTH AMERICAN DESIGNS

T HE INDIGENOUS PEOPLES OF North and South America already had their own highly developed decorative crafts before the arrival of the Europeans in the early sixteenth century. Native American baskets, woven blankets and rugs, buffalo-hide robes, pottery, beadwork and other artefacts were often decorated with symmetrical, boldly geometric designs. The European settlers' steely, thrifty inventiveness combined with the influences of their homelands to produce delightful designs for stenciling, carving, patchwork and other folk art. Farther south, the brilliantly colored textiles and pottery of Mexico reflect the influence of both the Aztecs and their Spanish conquerors, while the pre-Columbian textiles and ceramics of Peru depict the ancient myths and legends of the Incas.

PAINTED AND STENCILED CHAIR
The colorful bright red, blue, green and pink painted decoration on this chair was based on a Mexican embroidered blouse. All the wood on the chair was painted yellow, then the central flowers were stenciled, using one stencil for the green part, another for the outer petals and a third for the inner portion. The central yellow dots on each flower were stenciled last. The flowers flanking the central ones were stenciled in the same way. The birds were stenciled in blue, then the green wings and eyes stenciled separately. The stripes were painted by hand.

For flower-and-bird motif, see page 30 (no. 84).

For dog motif, see page 28 (no. 76)

APPLIQUÉ CUSHION

The appliquéd dog on this cushion originally appeared on an embroidered textile from Guatemala. Fabric squares (and one circle) were slipstitched to the dog shape cut out from yellow fabric, which was in turn slipstitched to backing fabric. Running stitch around the dog, plus braid edging, add definition.

For duck motif, see page 32 (no. 100)

KNITTED DUCK MOTIF

Sometimes stylized motifs capture more of the essence of what they are depicting than realistic interpretations do, and this is just as true of designs produced centuries ago as it is of modern work. This stylized duck motif came from a fragment of a textile woven in pre-Columbian Peru. It would make a fun design for a knitted sweater, or it could be worked in Swiss darning (duplicate stitch).

North and South American Designs

For abstract motif, see page 17 (no. 4)

BEADWORK RUNNER
Beadwork can be used to decorate flat pieces of fabric used as table runners, wall hangings, cushion covers, curtain tiebacks or evening bags. This abstract pattern was taken from an appliqué apron made by Native Americans from the Great Lakes region. Beads in two contrasting colors and shapes have been used.

For star motif, see page 23 (no. 41)

STENCILED BOX
Simple wooden items are ideal for stenciled folk-art designs, such as this star motif taken from an American woven Jacquard bedcover. The box itself was painted first, using red on the outside, yellow on the inside and light blue on the rim. A light blue star was stenciled on the front, followed by the oval ring and central star, both in yellow. Finally, dark blue-green was used to stencil a leaf spray on each point of the star, and a central four-pointed star.

6

7

8

9

10

11

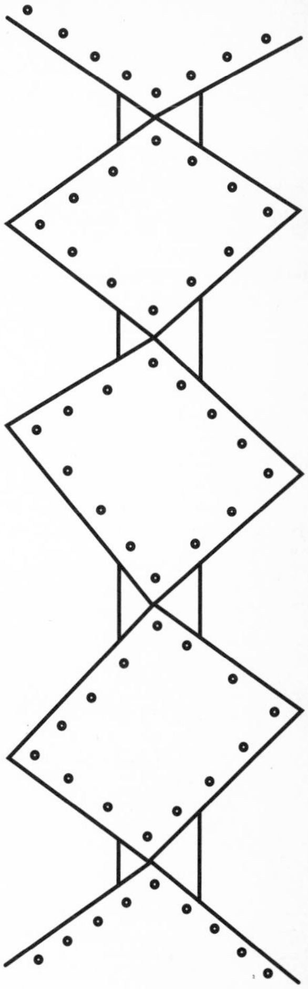

12

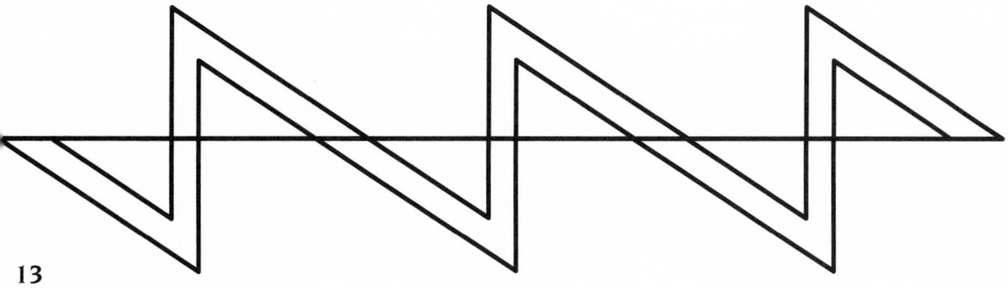

13

14

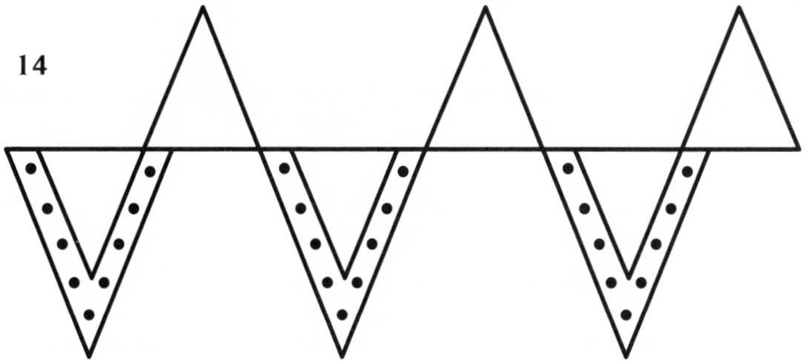

15

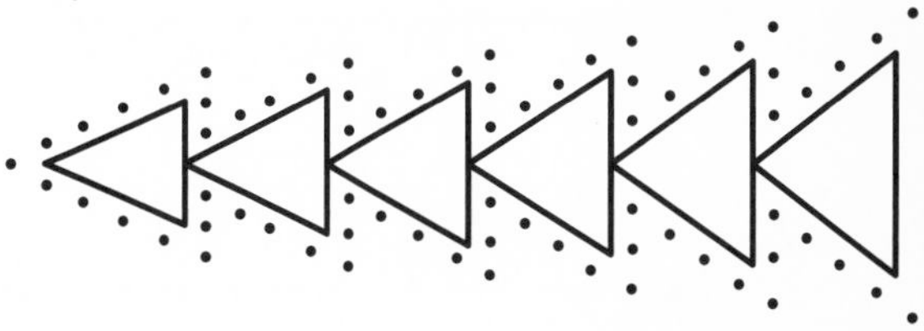

16

17

18

19

20

21

22

23

24

25

26

27

28

29

30

31

32   33   34

35

36

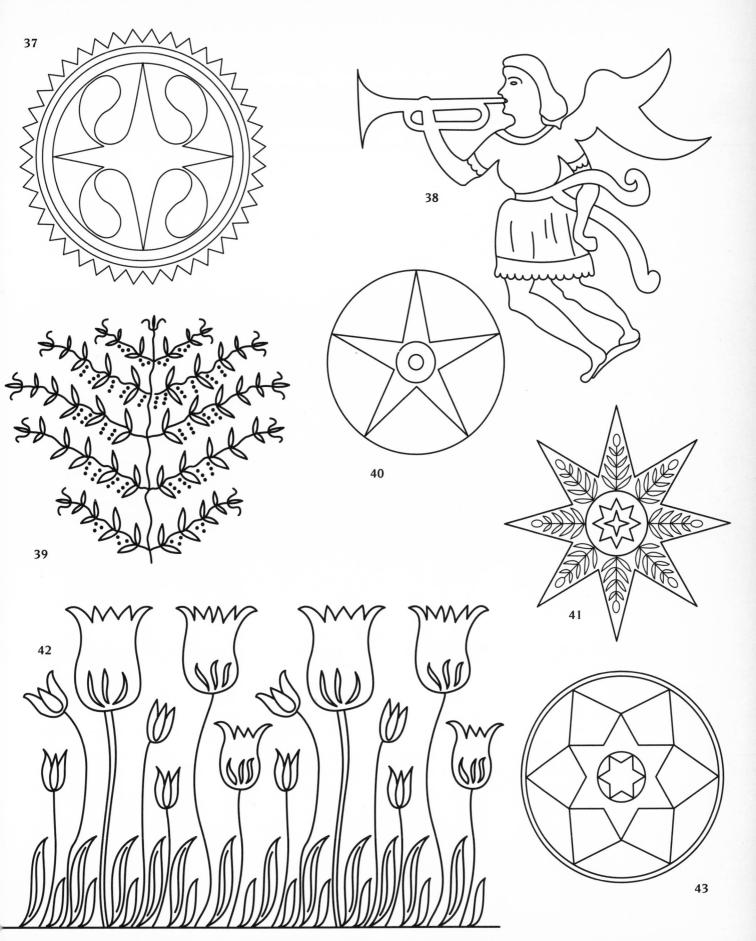

37

38

39

40

41

42

43

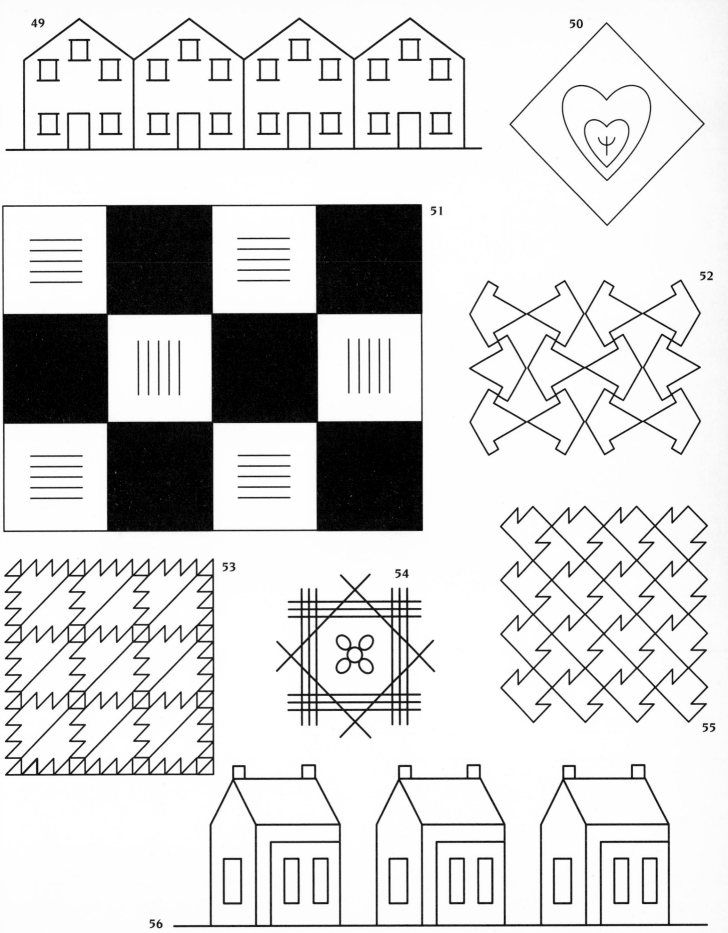

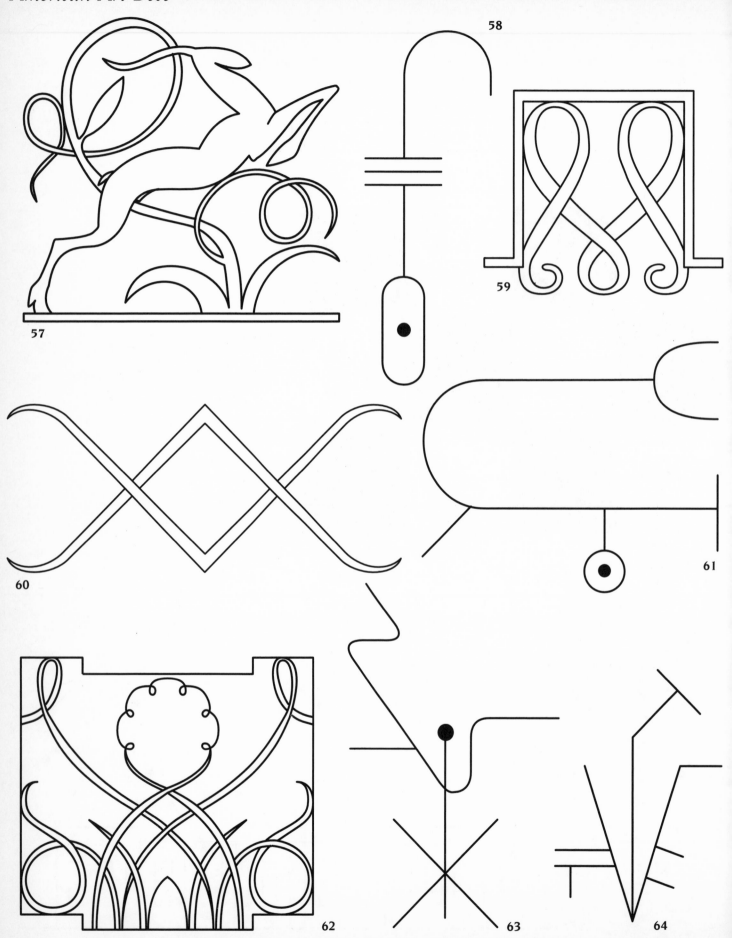

57

58

59

60

61

62

63

64

65

66   67   68

69   70

71

72

73

74

75

76

77

78

84

85

86

87

88

89

90

91

92

93

94

95

96

97

98

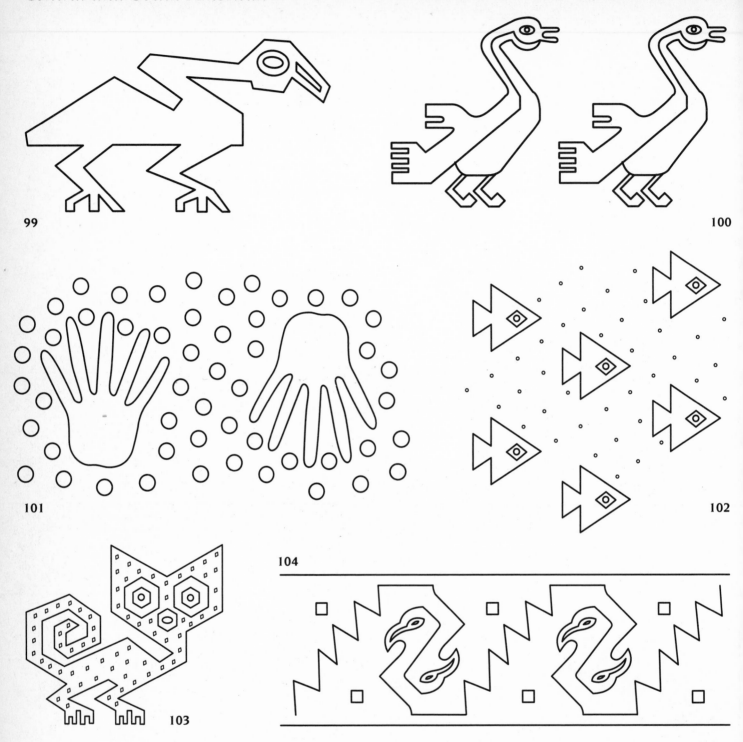

99

100

101

102

103

104

105

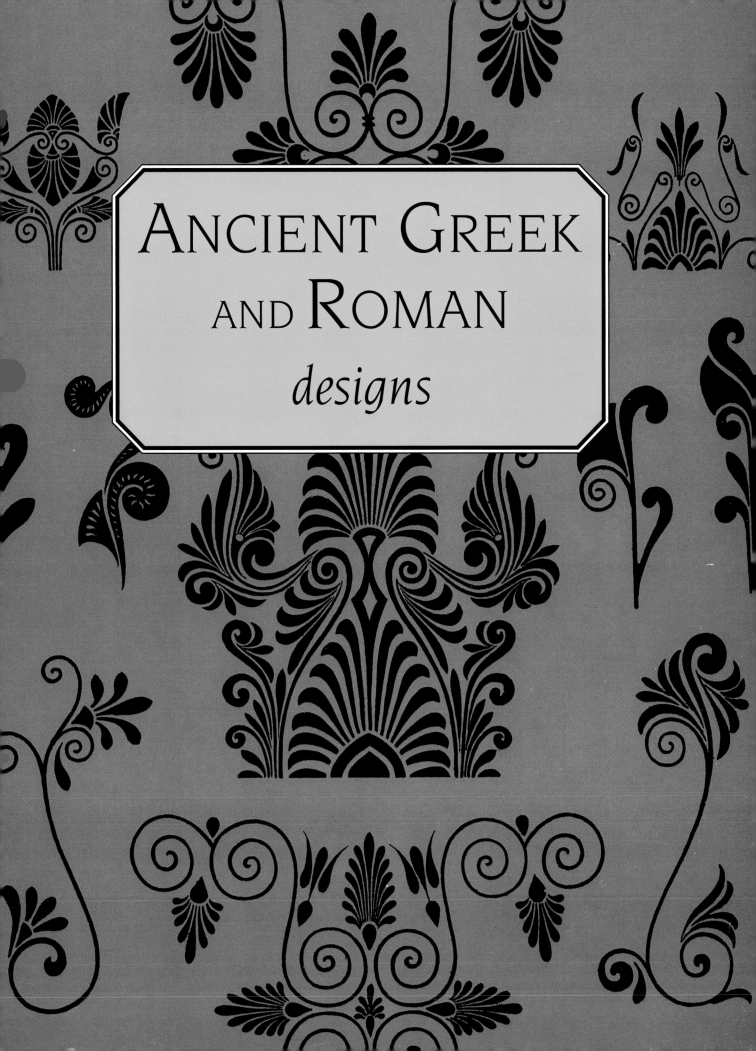

ANCIENT GREEK
AND ROMAN
designs

ANCIENT GREEK AND ROMAN DESIGNS

Even before the time of the ancient Greeks, the Minoan civilization on Crete was producing fine beaten metalwork, carved ivories, decorated pottery and superb frescoes. For the next thousand years, the ancient Greeks took ornament to a high degree of refinement and grace; many of their painted vases still survive today. In Italy, the Etruscans too were producing decorated pottery, mostly derived from Greek designs. Like the Greeks, they were eventually taken over by Rome. Greatly influenced by Greece, the Romans were responsible for passing on the wonderful legacy of classical ornament that has influenced architects, designers and decorators up to the present day.

For shape of scroll motif, see page 49 (no. 93)
For animal motifs, see pages 41 (no. 31, 33, 34), 43 (no. 45), 44 (no. 56) and 45 (no. 66)

PAINTED AND STENCILED
MINI-CHEST OF DRAWERS
The holes used to open the little drawers in this chest are part of the design. The scroll on the sides and top of the chest is widely used in classical ornament, while the animals on the drawers were taken from the border encircling an ancient Greek pot. The drawers were painted deep brown and the front of the chest in blue. To match this effect, the top, sides and back were painted in deep brown with blue around the edges. Next, a simplified scroll was stenciled in blue on the sides and top. The creatures on the drawers were hand-painted.

Ancient Greek and Roman Designs

For main border motif, see page 43 (no. 51)
For small, inner border motif, see page 42 (no. 42)

APPLIQUÉ TABLECLOTH

This lively, modern-looking design was actually taken from an ancient Greek vase. The simple shapes are ideal for appliqué and here have been cut out from plain cotton fabrics, with a small print for the central stripe. All the pieces have been slipstitched in place, and then a decorative running stitch worked near the edges.

PAINTED AND INCISED BOWL

The same design as on the tablecloth above has been painted onto this pottery bowl. Stenciling was used to create the dark outer shapes, and their 'mirror images' as beige outlines or orange shapes. Between these, lines were incised (scratched into the paint). Another, smaller border was hand-painted near the center.

35

Ancient Greek and Roman Designs

NEEDLEPOINT CUSHION
The stylized honeysuckle pattern used here was a common feature of both Greek and Roman decoration. Its simple, bold lines make it perfect for translating into needlepoint. The design was drawn on canvas and then worked in tent stitch using blue, white and black yarn. A narrow border in a contrasting color frames the image.

For honeysuckle motif, see page 43 (no. 48)

STENCILED FRIEZE
This glorious Roman border design is just right for stenciling, though it does require careful cutting, and precise matching of the repeats when stenciling. Only one stencil was used for all the colors. The three-dimensional effect was achieved by using strong, bright colors on the 'front' curves, making them stand out from the tones of the rest. After the border was completed, the small flowers and tiny squares were stenciled in the center.

For intertwining border motif, see page 47 (no. 79)

36

1

2

3

4

6

5

7

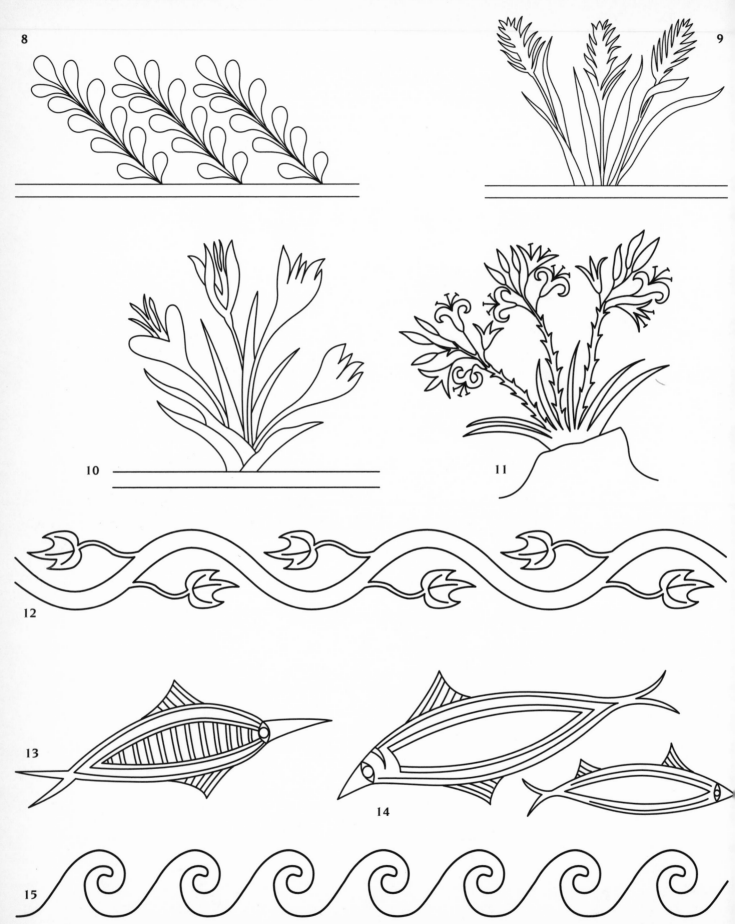

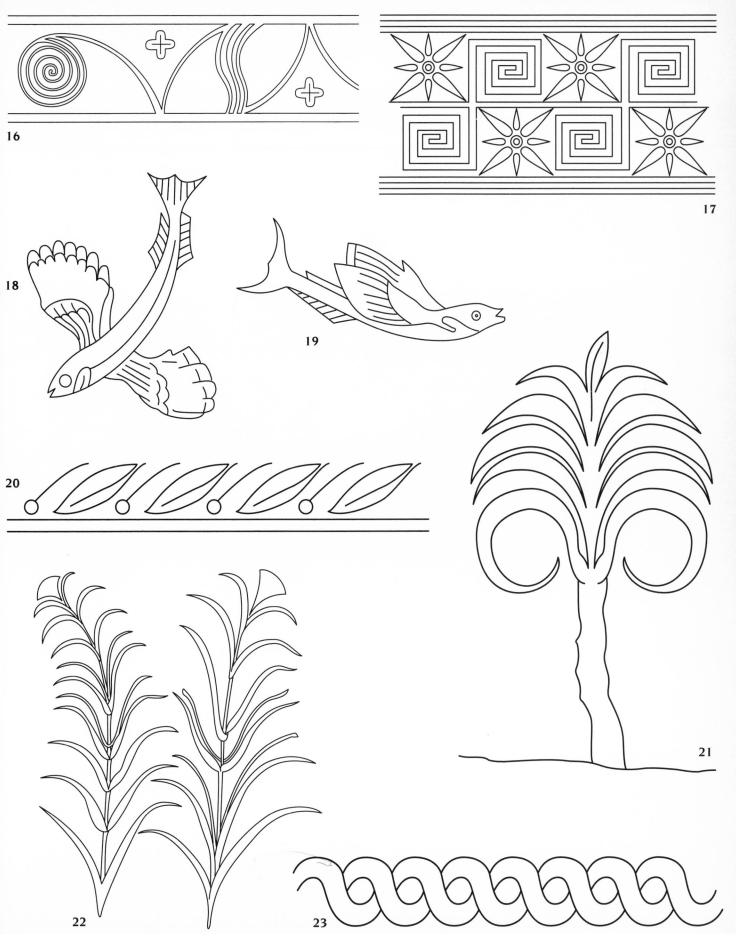

16

17

18

19

20

21

22

23

24

25

26

27

28

29

30

31

32

33

34

35

36

Ancient Greek

37

38

39

40

41

42

43

44

45

46

47

48

49

50

51

52

43

53

54

55

56

57

58

59

60

61

62

63

64

65

66

73

74

75

76

77

78

79

80

81

82

83

84

85

86

87

88

89

90

91

92

93

94

95

96

97

98

99

100

101

102

103

104

105

106

107

108

109

110

111

112

113

114

115

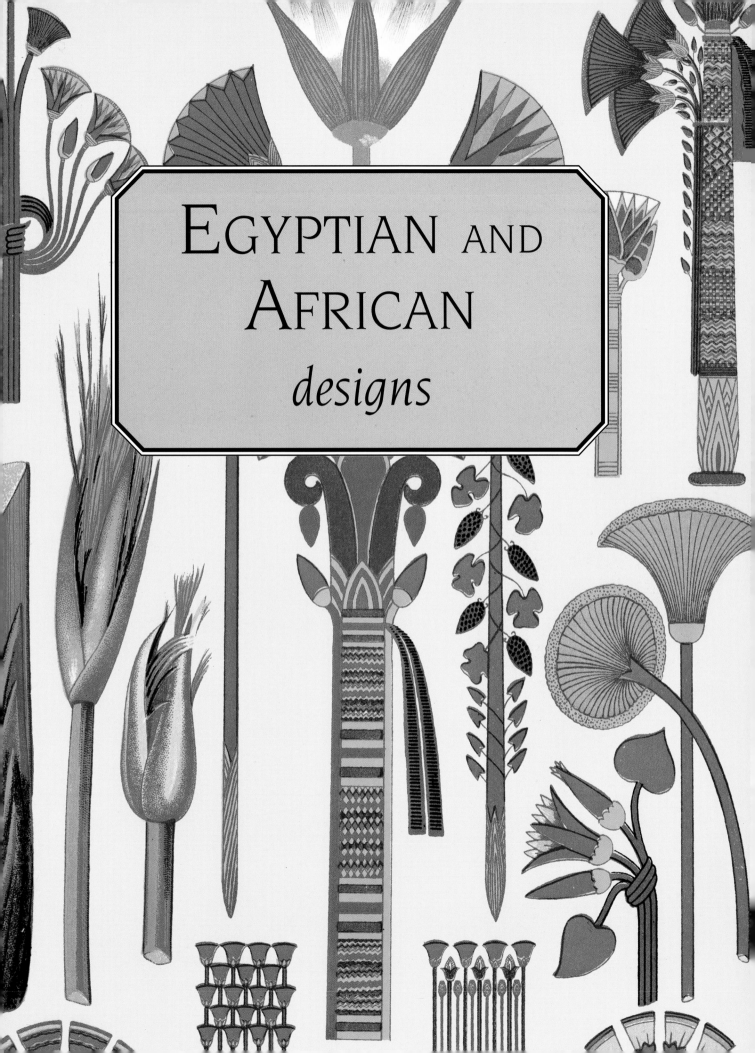

EGYPTIAN AND AFRICAN *designs*

EGYPTIAN AND
AFRICAN DESIGNS

THE DESIGNS OF EGYPT provide a glorious beginning to the decorative arts of this monumental continent. For about three thousand years before the birth of Christ, the ancient Egyptians produced paintings and carvings which they believed gave life or immortality to whatever was being represented. Many of the stylized natural forms, such as the lotus, papyrus and palmette motifs, were associated with the life-giving Nile.

The arts of Africa reflect the humor and ingenuity of its varied peoples, cultures and religions – at the same time highly sophisticated and delightfully straightforward. From the wall decoration of Morocco and Mauritania to the striking weaving and humorous appliquéd flags of Ghana, the designs are as inspirational as they are unique.

KNITTED CUSHION
Bright and graphic, this heart set against a background of uneven stripes is a very enlarged version of a design woven by Ashanti tribesmen in Ghana. Known as 'men's weaves', the designs include motifs such as hands, fish and swords, all against stripes. The combination of a simple but striking shape against stripes makes the design ideal for knitting. Here it is used for a cushion but it could easily be adapted to a knitted garment such as a sweater.

For heart-and-stripe motif, see page 71 (no. 100)

54

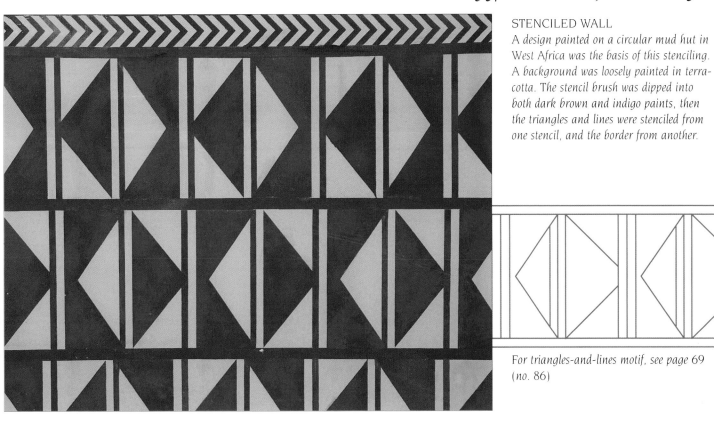

Egyptian and African Designs

STENCILED WALL

A design painted on a circular mud hut in West Africa was the basis of this stenciling. A background was loosely painted in terracotta. The stencil brush was dipped into both dark brown and indigo paints, then the triangles and lines were stenciled from one stencil, and the border from another.

For triangles-and-lines motif, see page 69 (no. 86)

STENCILED CUSHION

This fanciful stenciled cushion is based on an Asafo flag appliquéd by the Fanti people of Ghana. The people and jungle motifs have been arranged around the fabric in order to fill the entire square, with just one stencil used for all the colors. The colors were repeated in the stenciled border around the edge.

For jungle-and-people motif, see page 71 (no. 102)

Egyptian and African Designs

For leaf motif, see page 58 (no. 14)

HAND-PAINTED PAPIER MÂCHÉ BOX

A design based on a traditional Egyptian lotus flower is used to decorate this box. After adding the brown and yellow areas and the blue stripes, the flowers were hand-painted. They were rearranged to fit onto the top of the long, narrow box. A second, simpler lotus motif is used (upside down) as a border around the sides of the box.

For lotus stem motif, see page 58 (no. 15)

STENCILED TABLE

The exotic fish motif on this stenciled table was taken from an ancient Egyptian pottery bowl. After the yellow background was loosely painted, the design was added using two stencils — the first for the basic shape and the second for the details. The rim of the table and the stripes were painted by hand.

For fish motif, see page 57 (no. 6)

16

17

18

19

20

21

22

23

24

25

26

27

28

29

30

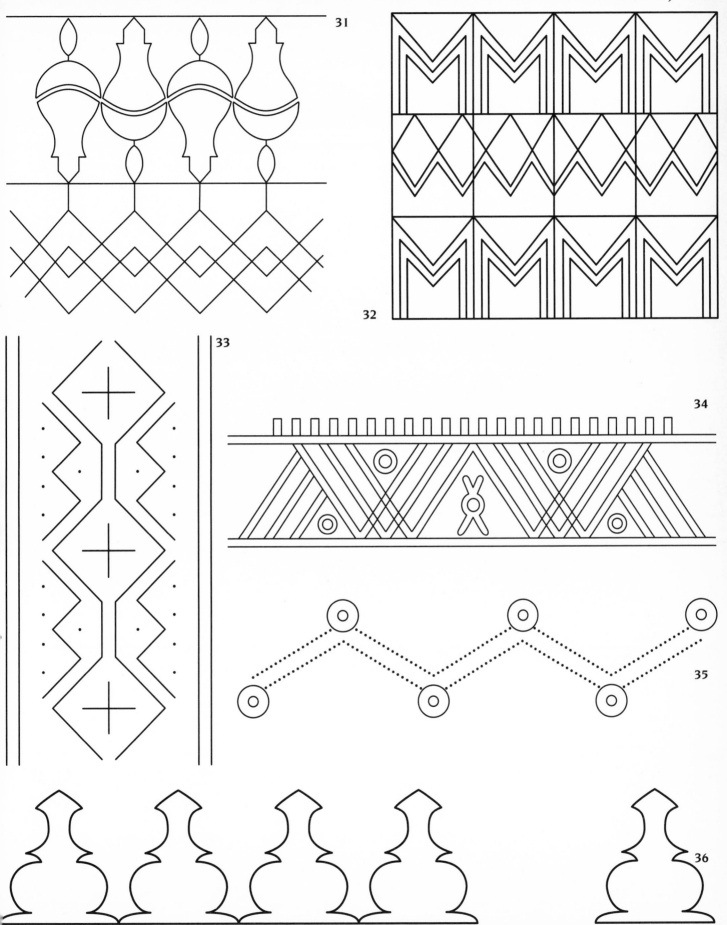

37

38

39

40

41

42

43

44

45

46

47

48

49

50

51

52

53

54

55

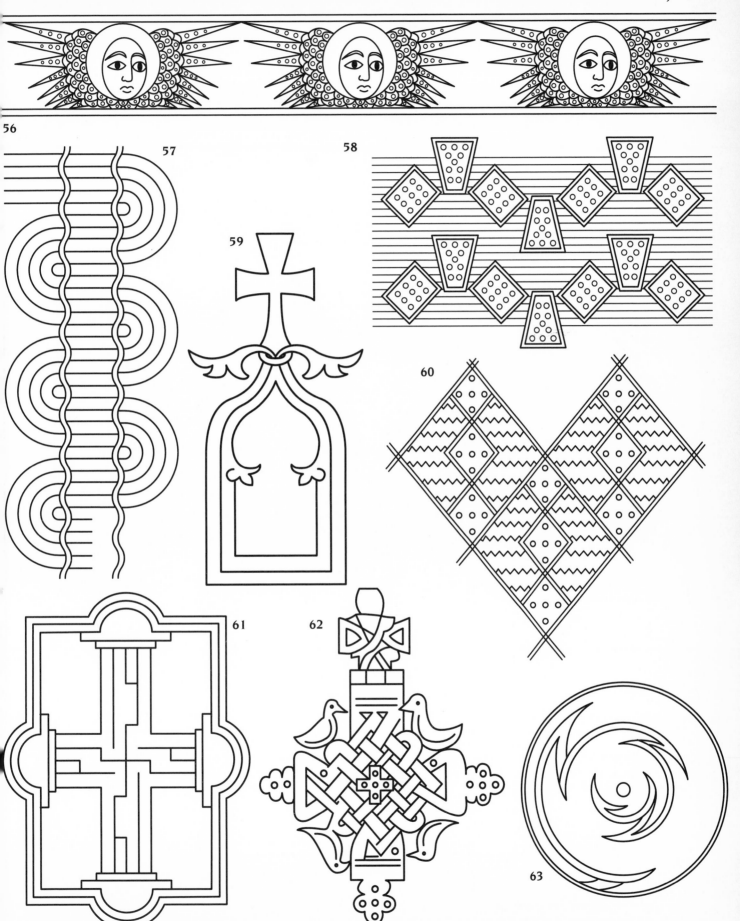

56

57

58

59

60

61

62

63

64

65

66

67

68

69

70

71

72

73

74

75

76

77

78

86

87

88

89

90

91

92

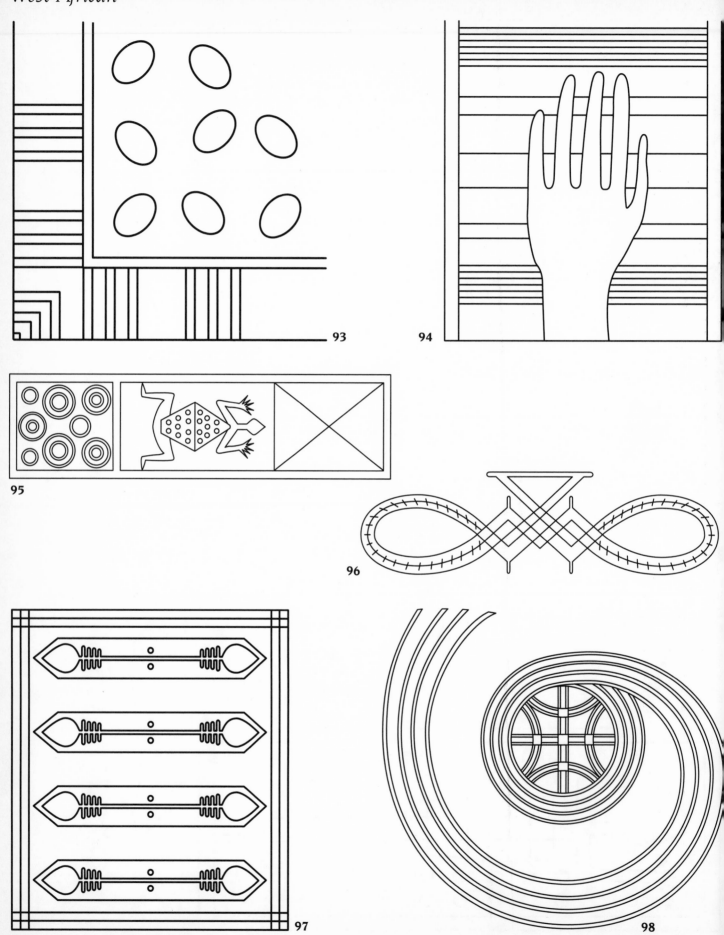

93

94

95

96

97

98

99

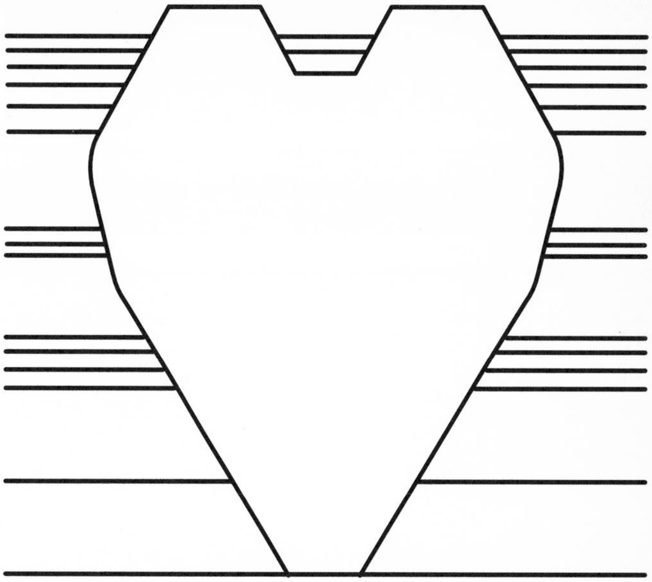

100

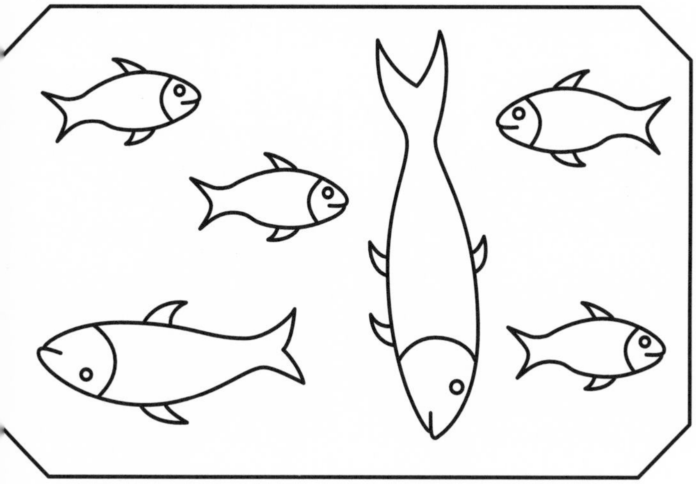

101

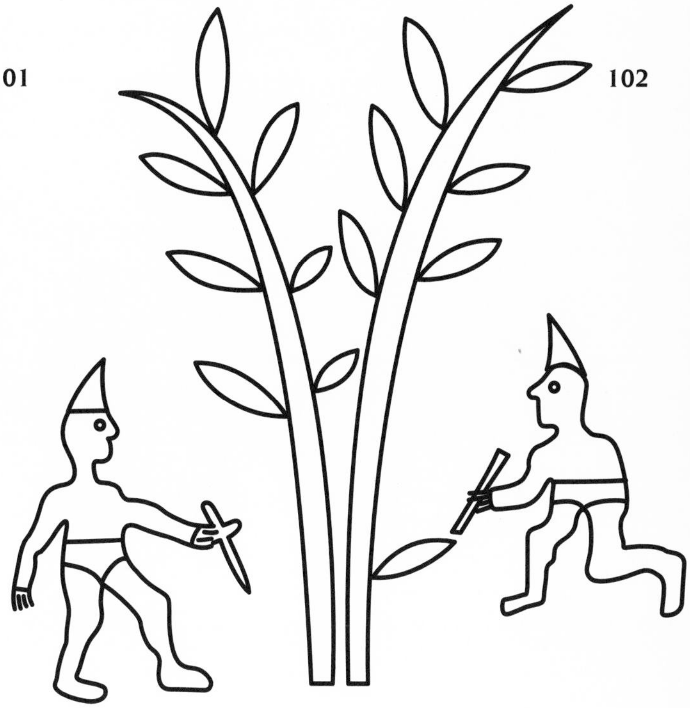

102

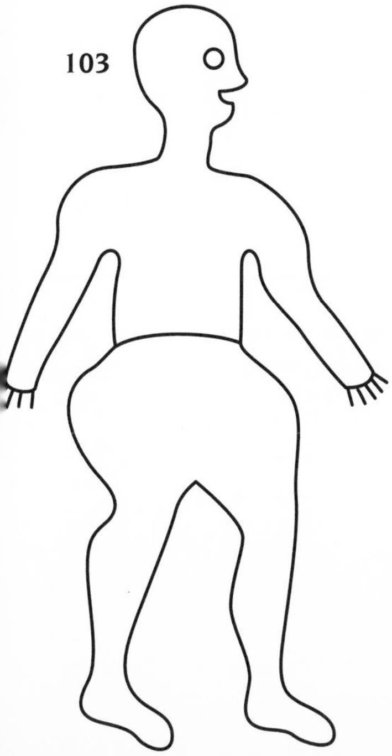

103

104

105

106

107

108

109

110

111

112

ORIENTAL
designs

ORIENTAL DESIGNS

THE ANCIENT SYMBOLS OF the Orient, combined with vibrant colors, make for powerful designs. Silks and porcelain, embellished with flowers and fruit, made their way out of China along the trade routes, influencing the world of design along the way. Many Far Eastern designs are full of symbolism and interwoven with their beliefs. For example, the pine, willow and bamboo, when they appear together, represent Buddha, Confucius and Lao-tzu.

The strict disciplines of the Japanese way of life have given rise to a wonderful inventiveness. Birds, fish, insects and plant life, both naturalistic and stylized, are used to great effect on textiles, lacquerwork and ceramics, all characterized by a quiet order and balance.

For cloud motifs, see page 80 (no. 28, 32)

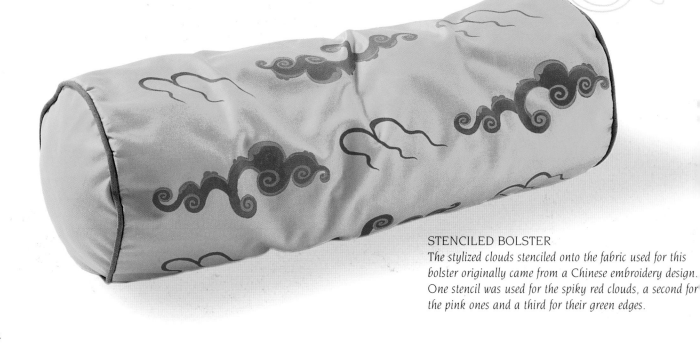

STENCILED BOLSTER
The stylized clouds stenciled onto the fabric used for this bolster originally came from a Chinese embroidery design. One stencil was used for the spiky red clouds, a second for the pink ones and a third for their green edges.

EMBROIDERED EVENING BAG

The Chinese 'endless knot' pattern was used for this embroidered evening bag, in which twisted embroidery threads in two colors were couched using contrasting, finer thread.

For endless-knot motif, see page 80 (no. 26)

STENCILED HAND MIRROR

This pretty wooden mirror was first painted and then stenciled with a design taken from an antique Korean pottery dish. One stencil was used for the small floral spray, and another for the central floral medallion. The teardrop-shaped 'holes' in the central flower were actually stenciled separately, in grey.

For floral-spray motif, see page 88 (no. 87)
For floral medallion motif, see page 86 (no. 71)

Oriental Designs

For fan motif, see page 82 (no. 45)

83 - 52

PATCHWORK AND APPLIQUÉ THROW
This fan design is from a Japanese Noh costume. Strips of silk in muted colors were first stitched together to form a patchwork fabric, and then the curved shapes were cut from them. The fans were appliquéd to the silk fabric, and silk ribbon was slipstitched over the edges.

PAPIER MÂCHÉ PITCHER
A design taken from a Chinese pottery bowl decorates this pitcher. After the pitcher was painted, the flowerheads were cut out from colored paper and pasted on, then the stems and leaves were painted onto the surface. Finally, the whole surface was given several coats of varnish.

For tulip motif, see page 80 (no. 31)

1

2

3

4

5

6

7

8

17

18

19

20

21

22

23

24

25

26

27

28

29

30

31

32

33

34

35

36

37

38

39

40

41

42

43

44

45

46

47

64

65

66

67

68

70

69

71

72

73

74

75

76

77

78

79

80

88

89

90

91

92

93

Indonesian

Tmas
Tree
Skirt

94

95

96

97

98

99

90

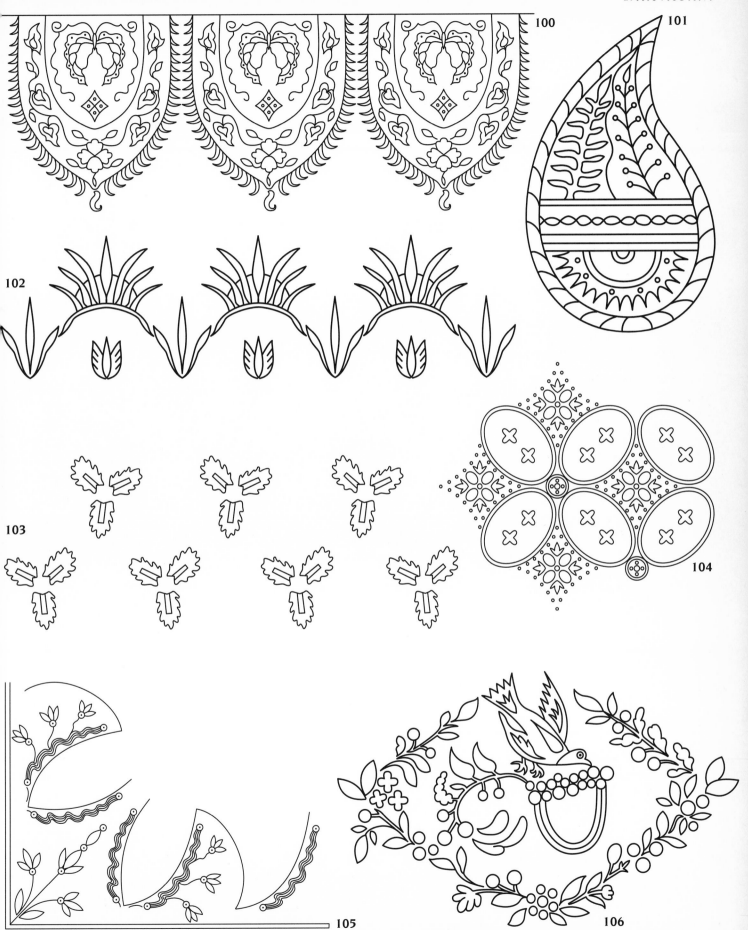

100

101

102

103

104

105

106

107

108

109

110

111

112

113

114

MEDITERRANEAN
designs

MEDITERRANEAN DESIGNS

THE LANDS OF SUN and siestas, olive trees and wine have rich decorative traditions. In France these range from country pottery and Provençal prints to toile de Jouy fabrics and rococo plasterwork. In Italy the flamboyant decorations of the Renaissance created a joyful spirit – a tradition that has survived up to modern times, for example in the designs of the Memphis group or the embroideries of Versace. The character of Spain has been molded by both Catholicism and Islam. From the painted roof beams of medieval Catalan churches to the intricate patterning on colored tiles, Spain, like the entire Mediterranean region, is a truly varied source of inspiration.

HAND-PAINTED
MIRROR FRAME
*Originally embroidered on
eighteenth-century velvet
curtains in France, this
rococo-like border was first
transferred to the green
painted background using
a ruler for straight lines. It
was then hand-painted in
blue, with white highlighting and grey shading. The
edges of the frame were
also hand-painted.*

*For the rococo border motif,
see page 98 (no. 8)*

For *flower motif, see page 103 (no. 44)*

APPLIQUÉ GLASSES CASE

This cheerful glasses case was inspired by an Italian pottery bowl, on which the design was repeated all the way around. Here the flower petals and the black scalloped borders have been cut from cotton and appliquéd to wool, with black machine satin stitch covering the raw edges. Very narrow black ribbon was stitched along the base of each motif to emphasize the lines.

For olive and oak branches motif, see page 106 (no. 69)

DÉCOUPAGE ALBUM COVER

A wall painting in an Italian castle was the basis for this album cover. Each stem, leaf, olive and acorn as well as the title banner, was cut out from paper and pasted on. For an album, a practical alternative to varnishing is to cover it with self-adhesive plastic film.

Mediterranean Designs

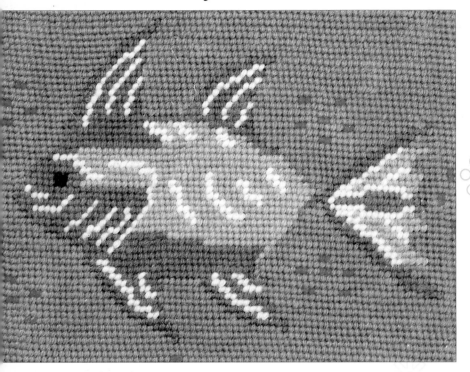

For fish motif, see page 111 (no. 105)

NEEDLEPOINT PICTURE
This realistic-looking fish originally came from a Portuguese pottery dish. It was worked here in tent stitch, using tan, red and white and two shades of green. As well as a picture, it could be used as a cushion cover.

STENCILED TRAY
Part of a motif taken from old Spanish lace has here been stenciled onto a tray. The wooden tray was first painted black, and two thin green lines painted around the lip. The woman was then stenciled onto it in white, with the grey detailing of her skirt added using a second stencil. Inside the inner green line, a red zigzag border was stenciled, and small stars were stenciled all over in white.

For woman-and-stars motif, see page 108 (no. 86)

16

17

18

19

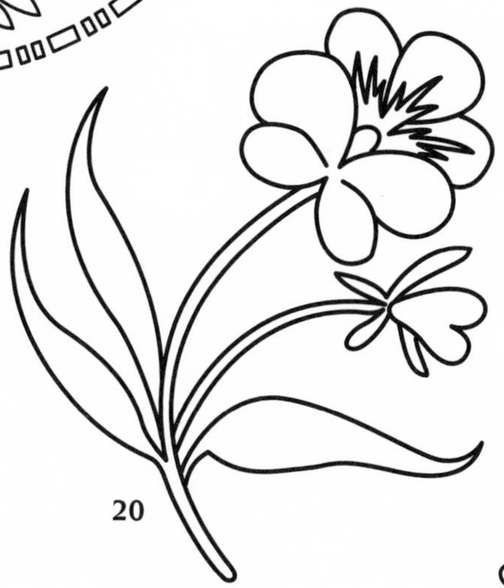

20

21

22

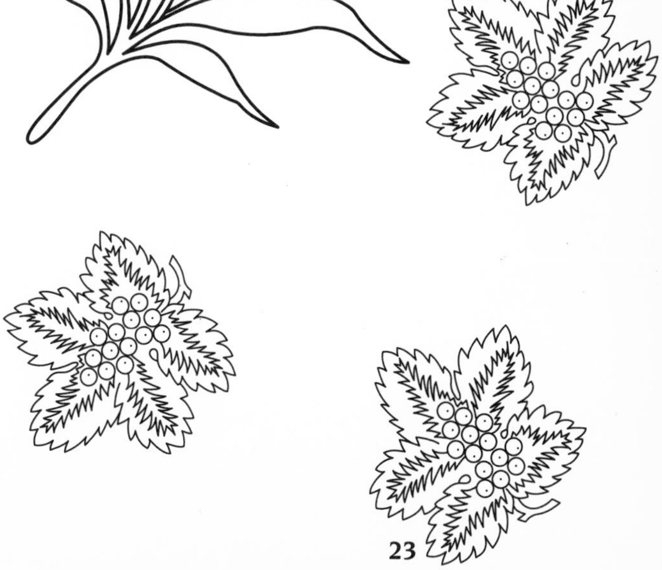

23

French

24

25

26

27

28

29

30

31

32

33

34

35

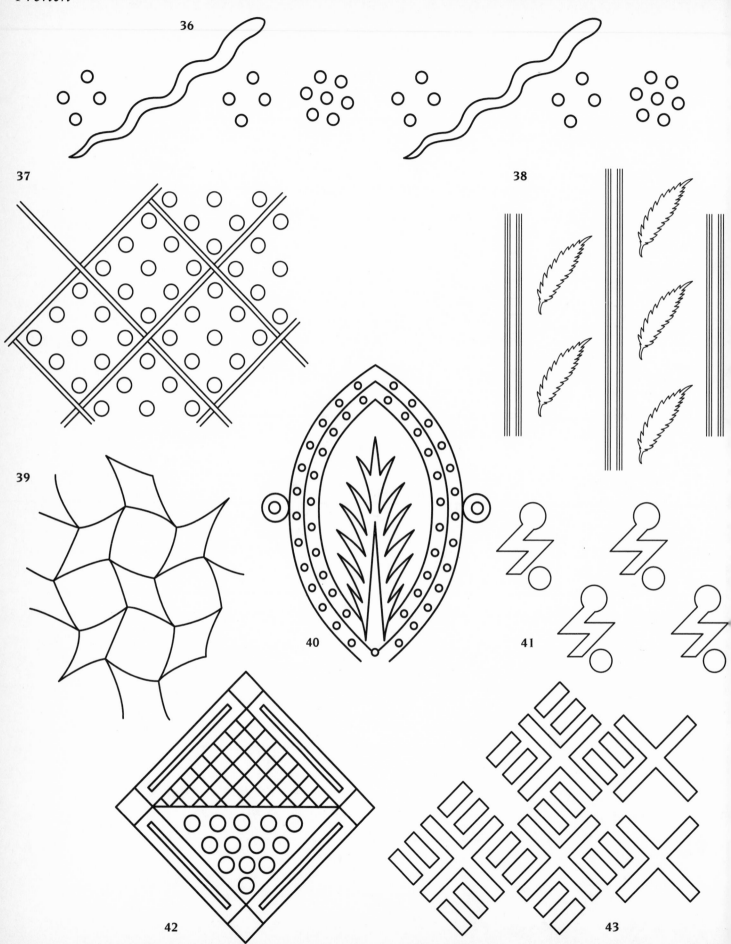

44

45

46

47

48

49

50

51

52

53

54

55

56

57

58

60

59

61

62

63

Italian

71

72

73

74

75

76

77

78

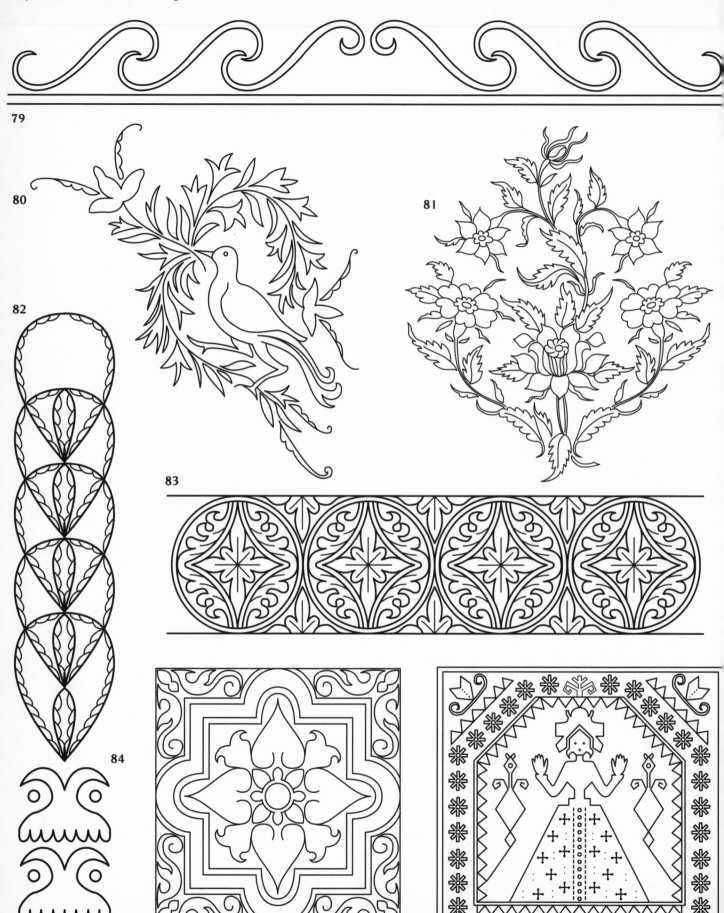

79

80

81

82

83

84

85

86

87

88

89

90

91

92

93

Spanish and Portuguese

94

95

96

97

98

99

100

101

102

103

104

105

106

107

108

109

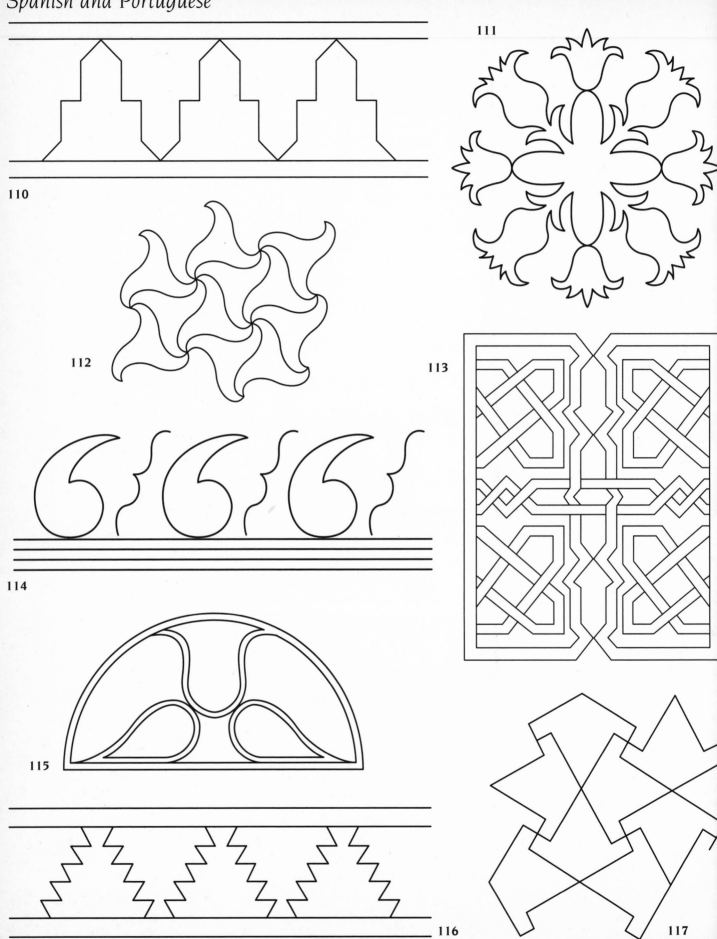

110

111

112

113

114

115

116

117

SCANDINAVIAN
designs

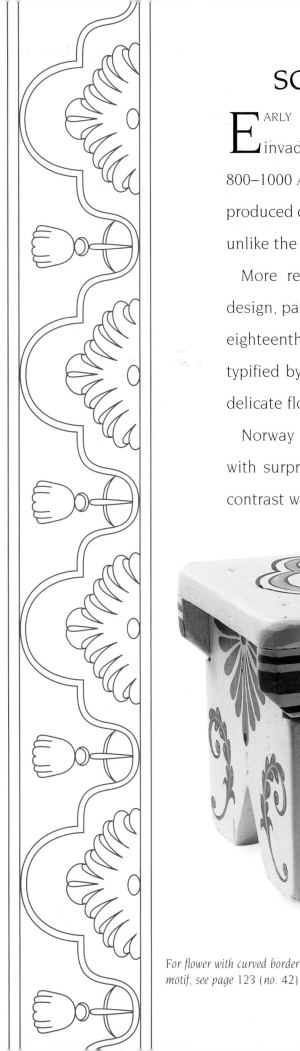

SCANDINAVIAN DESIGNS

Early inhabitants of Scandinavia, the warlike Vikings invaded Denmark, England and Northern Europe in 800–1000 AD. In spite of their fierce and brutal nature, they produced delicate gold and bronze incised decorations not unlike the intertwining patterns of the Celts.

More recently, the great attraction of much Swedish design, particularly that of the Gustavian period in the late eighteenth century, has been its soft simplicity of pattern – typified by demurely painted panels, with a powdering of delicate flowers.

Norway has excelled in strong, well-balanced designs with surprisingly bright and cheerful colors – perhaps to contrast with the pastel shades of the watery sunshine.

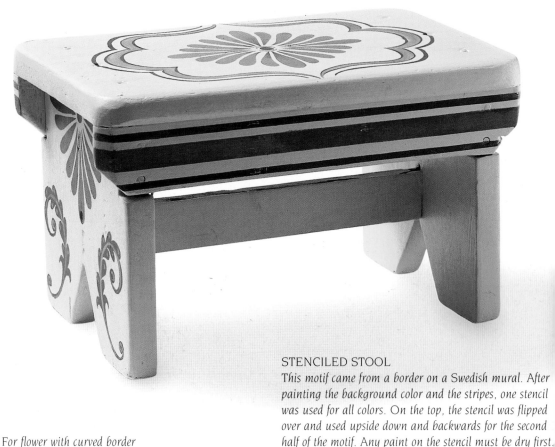

For flower with curved border motif, see page 123 (no. 42)

STENCILED STOOL
This motif came from a border on a Swedish mural. After painting the background color and the stripes, one stencil was used for all colors. On the top, the stencil was flipped over and used upside down and backwards for the second half of the motif. Any paint on the stencil must be dry first. Additional decoration, such as the blue foliage, can be added.

KNITTED MITTENS
These charmingly simple motifs were originally embroidered in silk on gloves from southern Sweden, but the design can easily be adapted for knitting. A similar effect could be created using Swiss darning (duplicate stitch) on purchased mittens.

For cross, flower and heart motifs,
see page 124 (no. 49, 50 and 51)

STAMPED OVAL BOX
A very old hand-painted frieze in a Swedish bedroom was the source of this stamped design. Light and dark pinks (for flowers) and mid- and yellow-green (for leaves) were brushed unevenly onto a high-density sponge stamp before each impression, to create a rough, uneven effect. A second sponge was used for the yellow-green circles.

For flower motif, see page 126 (no. 65)

Scandinavian Designs

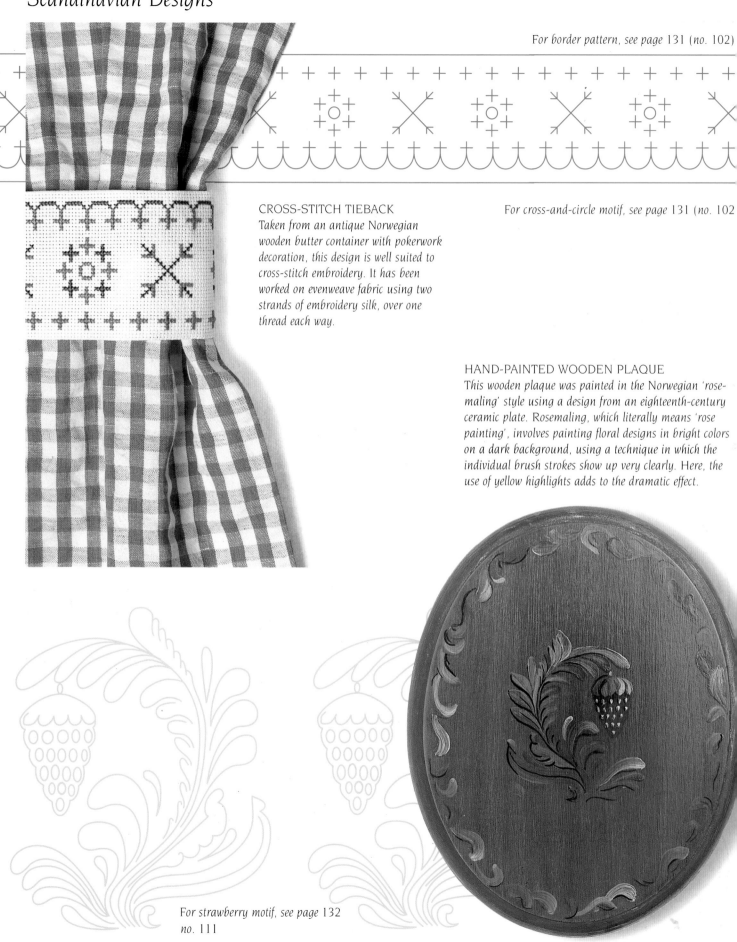

For border pattern, see page 131 (no. 102)

CROSS-STITCH TIEBACK

Taken from an antique Norwegian wooden butter container with pokerwork decoration, this design is well suited to cross-stitch embroidery. It has been worked on evenweave fabric using two strands of embroidery silk, over one thread each way.

For cross-and-circle motif, see page 131 (no. 102

HAND-PAINTED WOODEN PLAQUE

This wooden plaque was painted in the Norwegian 'rosemaling' style using a design from an eighteenth-century ceramic plate. Rosemaling, which literally means 'rose painting', involves painting floral designs in bright colors on a dark background, using a technique in which the individual brush strokes show up very clearly. Here, the use of yellow highlights adds to the dramatic effect.

For strawberry motif, see page 132
no. 111

1

2

3

4

5

6

15

16

17

18

19

20

21

Swedish

22

23

24

25

26

27

28

29

30

31

32

33

34

Swedish

35

36

37

38

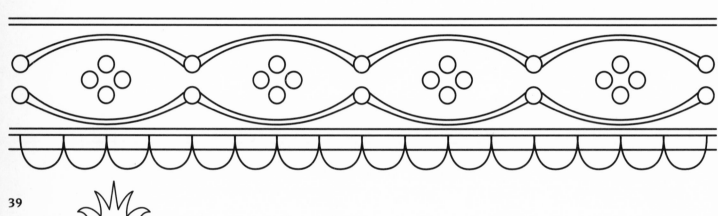

39

40

41

122

42

43

44

45

46

47

48

49

50

51

52

53

54

55

56

57

58

59

60

61

62

63

64

65

66

67

68

69

70

71

72

73

74

75

76

77

78

86

87

88

89

90

91

92

93

94

95

96

97

98

99

100

101

102

103

104

105

106

107

Norwegian

108

109

110

111

112

113

114

CELTIC AND BRITISH
designs

CELTIC AND BRITISH DESIGNS

ROM THE ENTANGLED CURVILINEAR designs of the Celts to the wonderfully naturalistic patterns of William Morris and beyond, British design offers an incredibly diverse range of pattern. The art of the Celts – the indigenous peoples of West Central Europe, who first invaded Britain in about 250 BC – dates back to the fifth century BC. It reached its pinnacle in the seventh century AD, with exquisite illuminated manuscripts and intricately decorated metalwork. During the Middle Ages the Church was the main artistic influence, while highlights of later centuries include Jacobean crewelwork, Georgian silk weaving and patterned china – all uniquely British in their elegance.

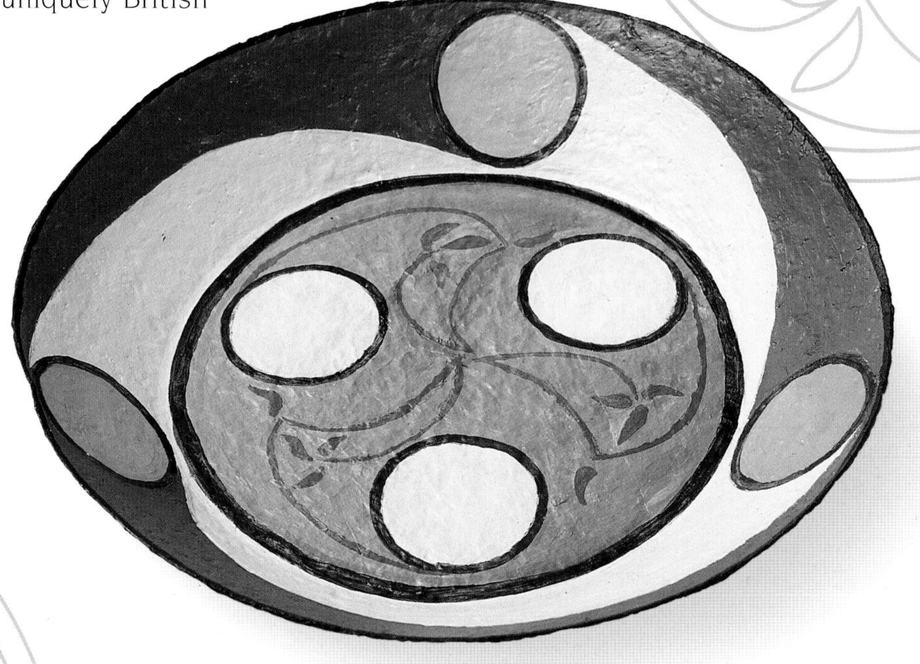

HAND-PAINTED PAPIER MÂCHÉ BOWL
Looking as dramatically modern as any pottery available today, this striking papier mâché bowl has been hand-painted with a design that is 1,300 years old. It is a detail from The Book of Lindisfarne, an Irish illuminated manuscript from the late seventh century. The outer portion of the design is an enlarged version of the inner portion. The bowl was first painted white, then the pink and yellow circles were filled in. When dry, the green tracery was painted onto the pink circle and the same green used around the edge. Finally, dark brown outlines were added.

For circle-and-tracery motif, see page 137 (no. 4)

For quatrefoil motif, see page 137 (no. 3)

STENCILED WALL

Celtic motifs such as this quatrefoil design, based on a pattern used in Celtic enamelwork, look wonderful stenciled as repeat patterns on walls or floors. All the colors were applied using one stencil, apart from the individual pink circles, which were produced with a separate stencil. On the main motif, olive green gradually blends into mustard, which becomes light pink, to create a softer, more varied effect.

EMBROIDERED CUSHION

What could be simpler than these circles embroidered in two colors on linen using French knots? The design is a simplified version of a background pattern in an illuminated Bible from nearly a thousand years ago — yet its use here is ideally suited to today's pared-down interiors.

For circles motif, see page 139 (no. 13)

Celtic and British Designs

For leafy motif, see page 143 (no. 43)
For acorn border motif, see page 143 (no. 38)

KNITTED CAP
The leaf design on the crown of this knitted cap is taken from a seventeenth-century English crewelwork bedcover, and the acorn border comes from an eighteenth-century English sampler. The stems and veins on the leaves were embroidered, echoing the designs' origins, and were worked, appropriately enough, in stem stitch.

STENCILED EMPIRE-STYLE SCARF
Three different motifs have been combined on this stenciled muslin scarf. All were taken from late eighteenth-century waistcoats made of figured silk from Spitalfields, London. One stencil and one color were used for each motif.

For large-leaved motif, see page 145 (no. 54)
For small-leaved motif, see page 145 (no. 56)
For leaf-and-circle border motif, see page 146 (no. 58)

12

13

14

15

16

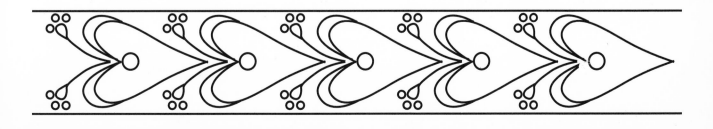

17

18

19

20

21

22

Medieval

30

31

32

33

34

35

36

37

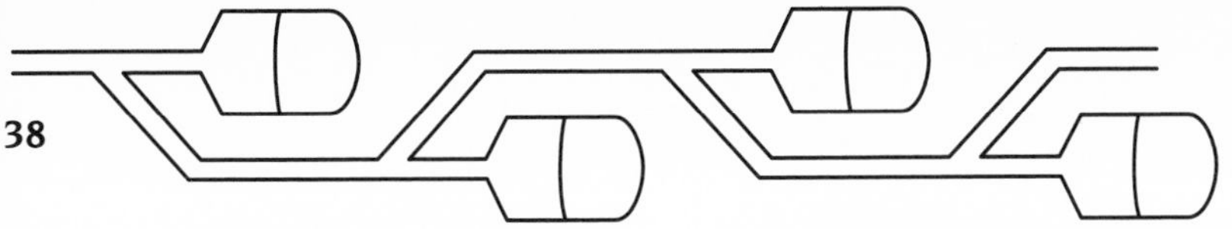

38

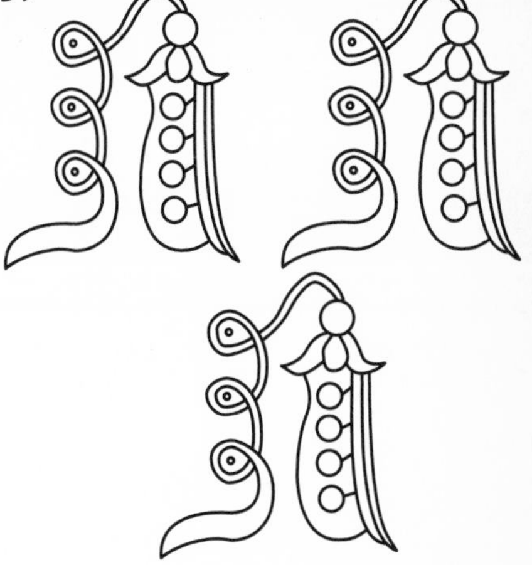

39

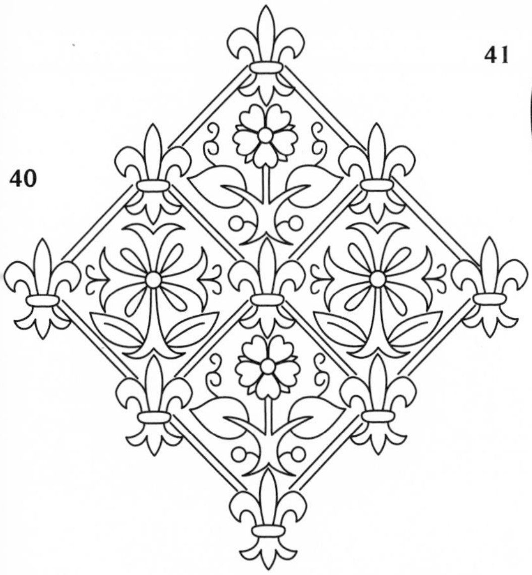

40

41

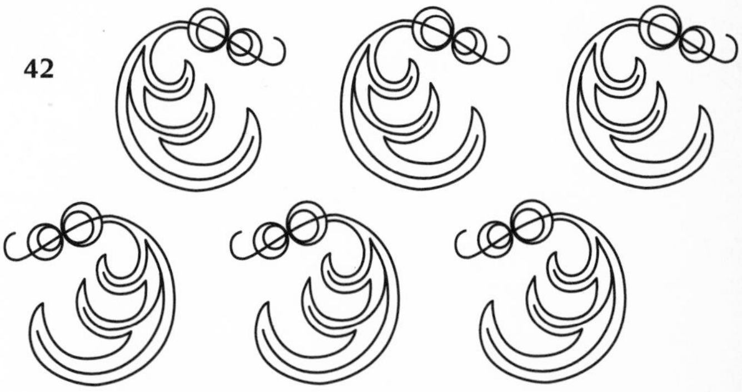

42

43

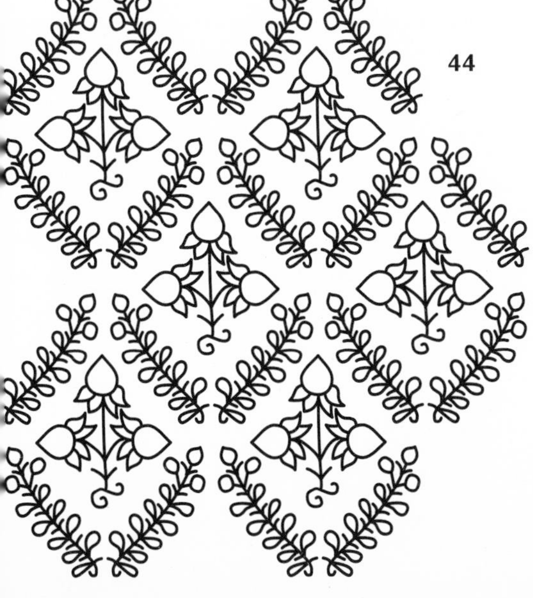

44

45

46

47

48

49

50

51

52

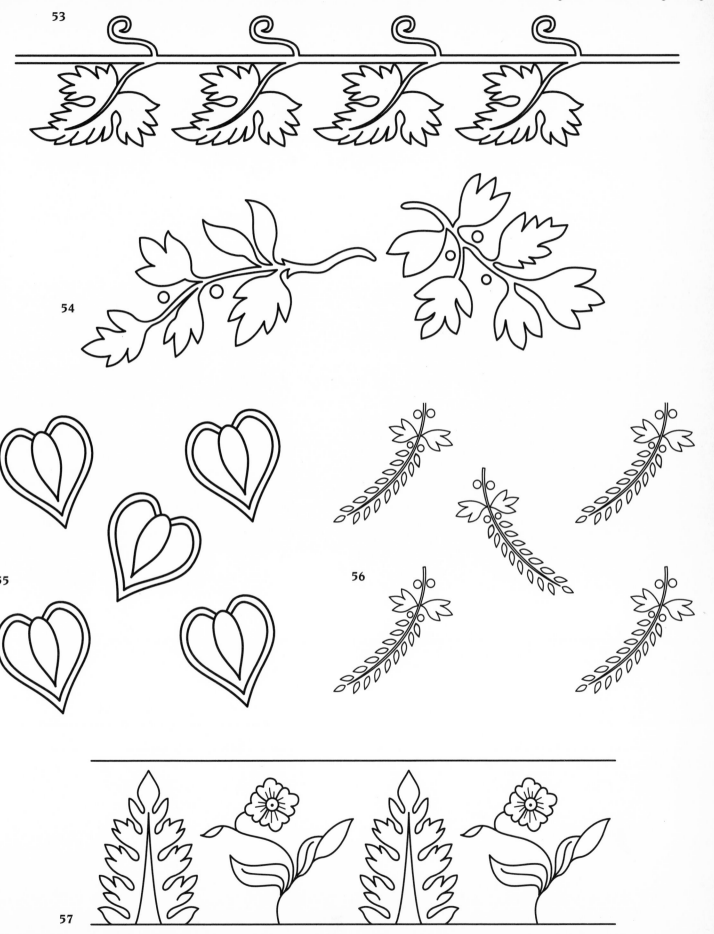

53

54

55

56

57

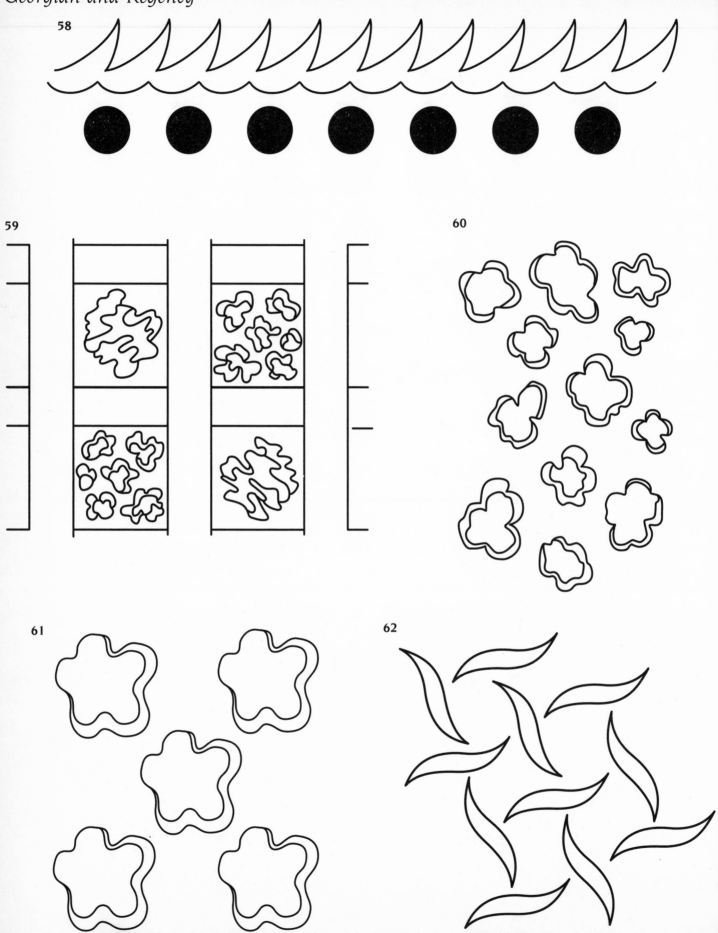

58

59

60

61

62

63

64

65

66

67

68

69

70

Victorian

71

72

73

74

75

76

77

78

148

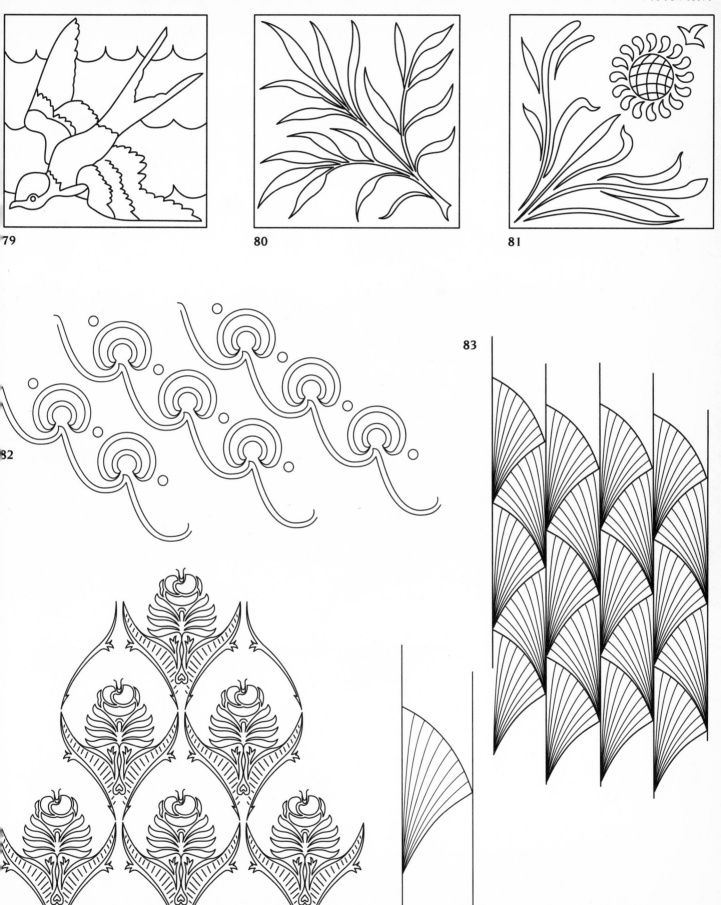

79

80

81

82

83

84

85

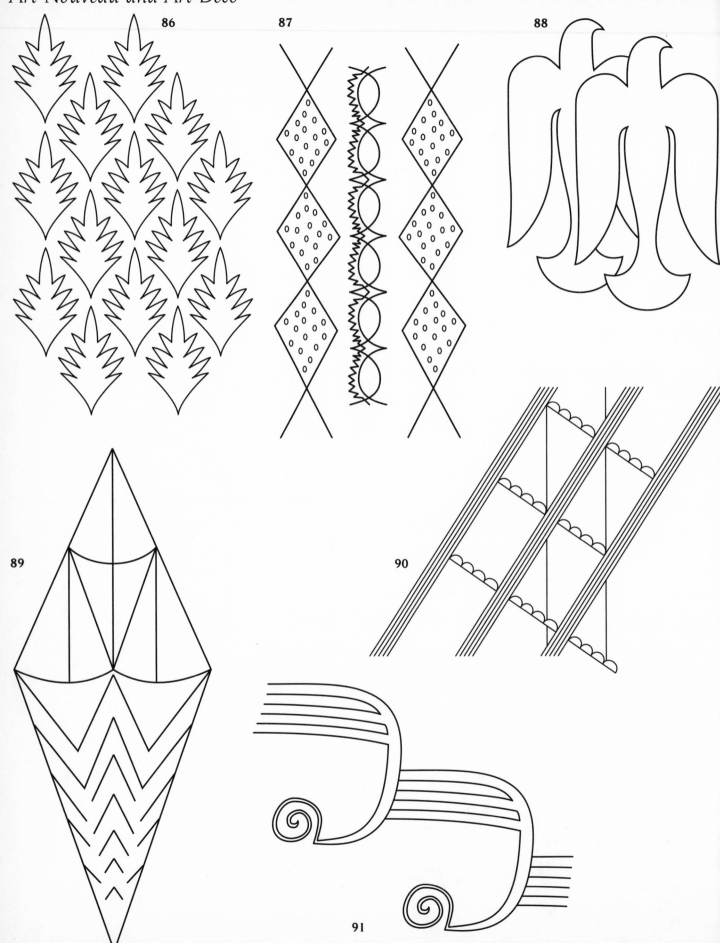

86

87

88

89

90

91

92

93

94

95

96

97

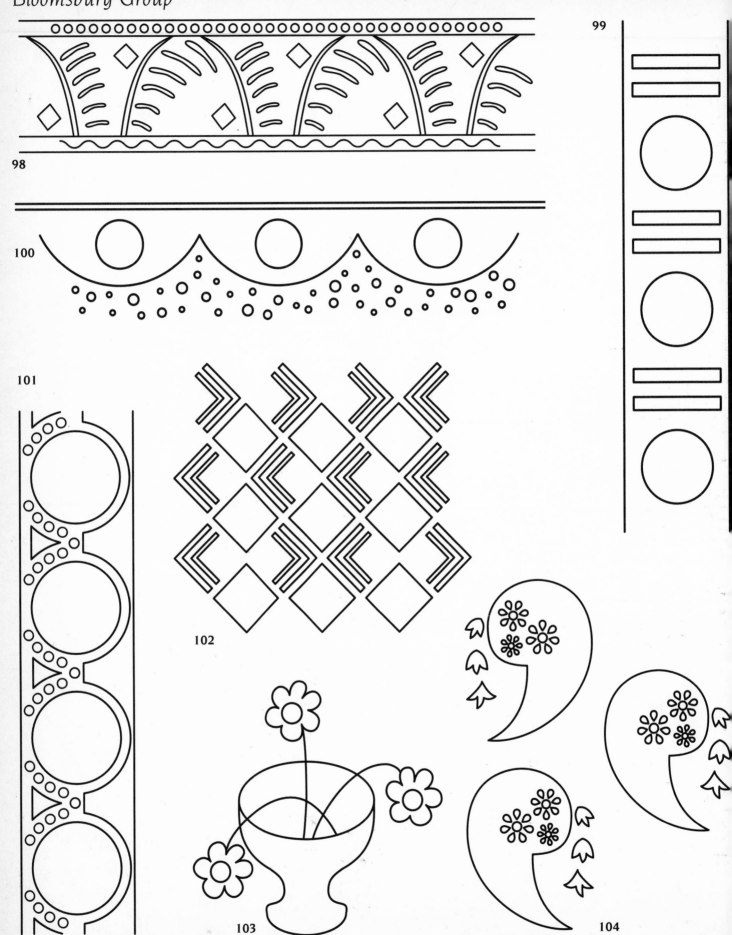

98

99

100

101

102

103

104

NORTHERN EUROPEAN
designs

NORTHERN EUROPEAN DESIGNS

ORTHERN EUROPE HAS A rich and varied folk-art tradition. Country people have covered many a wall and wooden surface with their exuberant painted decoration, and woodcarving, metalwork and needlecrafts were also widely used. In Poland glass was decorated, in Moravia eggs were painted, and in Hungary there was a decorated object for every occasion. Many of these traditions influenced Austria's Wiener Werkstätte and Germany's Bauhaus, as well as Russia's Constructivist movement, in the early part of the twentieth century. In fact, the Northern European decorative tradition forms the basis of modern design as we know it today.

STENCILED BOX
An antique hand-painted German trunk provided the design for this stenciled box with hand-painted detailing. One stencil was used for the panel borders and a second for the flowers and leaves.

For floral panel motif, see page 159 (no. 15)

For reindeer, tree and geometric border motifs, see page 163 (no. 44)

SWISS-DARNED SWEATER

This design, borrowed from an antique engraved horn salt cellar made by Hungarian shepherds, would delight any child. The motifs, including the geometric border around the lower edge, are embroidered onto the sweater using Swiss darning (duplicate stitch).

CROSS-STITCH PIN CUSHION

For this oval pin cushion, cross stitch has been used to cover the fabric completely, in a manner similar to needlepoint. The design is based on an antique decorated egg from Moravia in the Czech Republic.

For decorated hearts motif, see page 164 (no. 53)

Northern European Designs

For stylized leaf border motifs, see page 171 (no. 100 and 101)

DÉCOUPAGE BUCKET

The embroidered decoration around the hem of a Russian woman's costume was the basis for this design. Here the red and green sections of the bucket were hand-painted, along with the black-and-yellow border between them and around the base. The red shapes were painted on yellow paper then cut out to leave a thin yellow edge. The remaining elements of the design were cut out from yellow and blue paper. All were glued in position, then the whole surface was given several coats of varnish.

For hen with scroll border motif, see page 168 (no. 84)

STENCILED TRAY

The design for this delightful tray comes from a Rumanian tile, but because the tray is not square, the scroll border has been omitted from the top and bottom. The design was applied using one stencil for the border and a second for the hen and dotty background. The hen's eye and patterning were painted by hand.

20

21

22

23

24

25

26

28

27

29

30

31

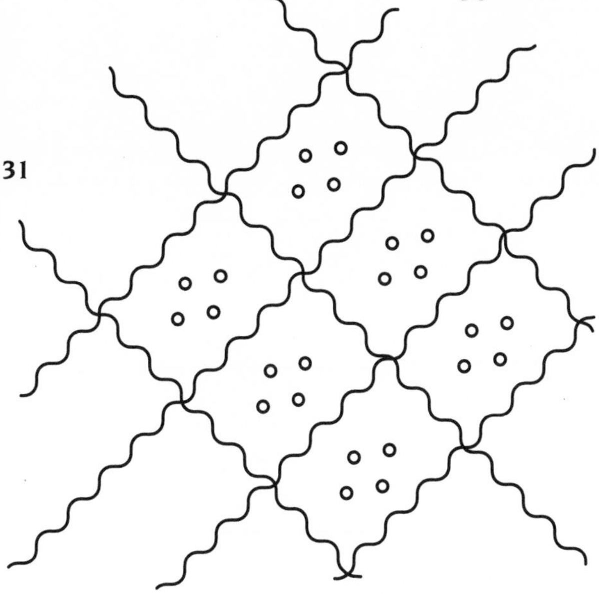

32

33

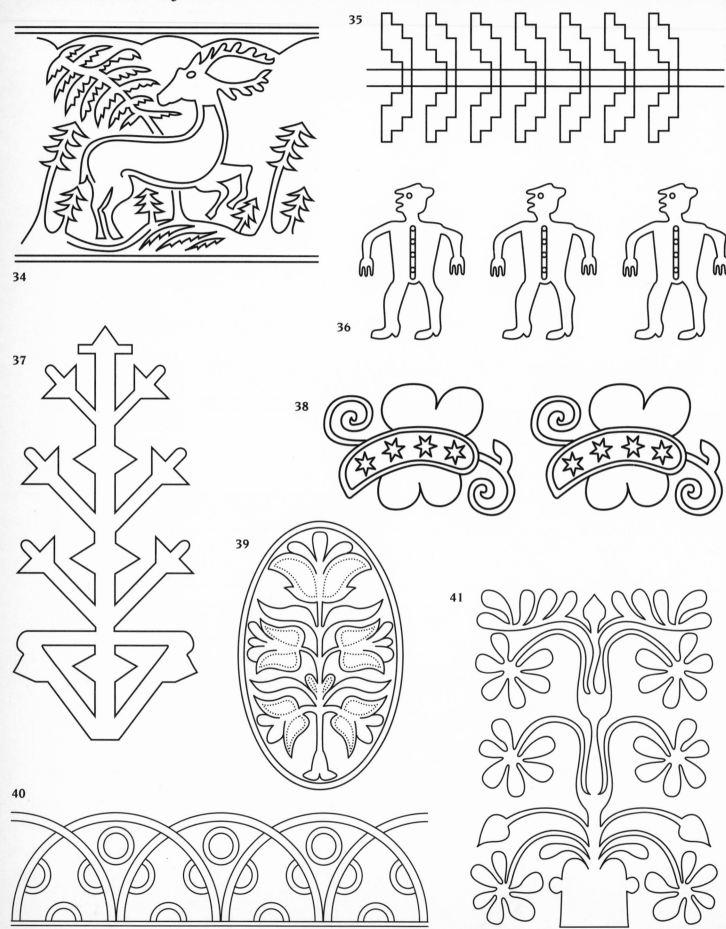

34

35

36

37

38

39

40

41

42

43

44

45

46

47

48

49

50

51

52

53

54

55

56

57

58

59

60

61

62

63

65

66

64

67

68

69

70

71

72

73

74

75

76

77

78

Rumanian

88

89

90

91

92

93

94

95

96

97

98

99

100

101

102

103

104

105

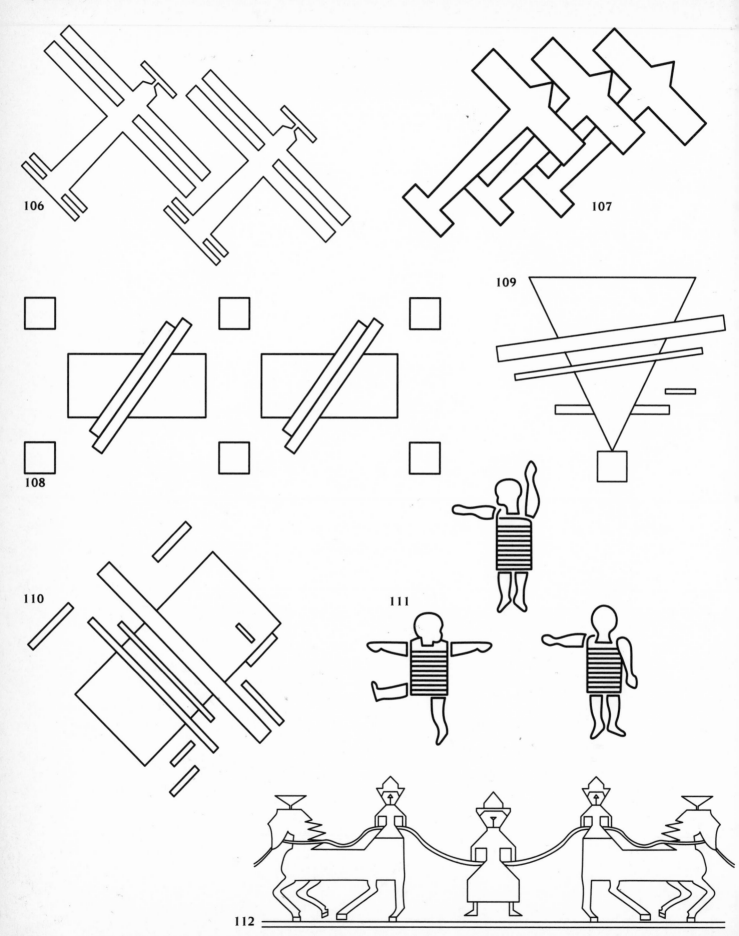

106

107

109

108

110

111

112

SOUTH ASIAN
designs

SOUTH ASIAN DESIGNS

I N INDIA AND PAKISTAN, pattern and color are everywhere, right down to drawings in the earth itself done to celebrate religious festivals. Virtually every surface is highly decorated. The subcontinent's long and varied history, as well as its range of cultures and religions, is reflected in its art forms, both past and present. In the famous Indian miniatures, there is a wealth of exquisite decorative detail. The joyful richness of the dress – jewelled turbans, patterned robes – is framed by intricately tiled palace walls, and then the images themselves are framed with twining, leafy floral borders or stripes of contrasting colors. Like many of the other art forms of this extraordinary subcontinent, these paintings provide a delectable source of pattern and inspiration.

STENCILED CABINET
The design for this stenciled cabinet comes from an antique textile from the Punjab. One stencil was used for the blue square and central dot, another for the flowers, a third for the corner dots and yellow border and a fourth for the outer border. The yellow flower centers were hand-painted.

For inner motif, see page 178 (no. 10)
For border motif, see page 188 (no. 94)

174

APPLIQUÉ BERET

The appliquéd design on this colorful felt beret came from a leather saddle cover used on camels in Hyderabad. Here, the shapes have been cut out from olive green cotton (plus yellow cotton for the small circles). They were appliquéd to the felt using yellow machine satin stitch to cover the raw edges.

For geometric border, see page 184 (*no. 52*)

For circular motif, see page 187 (*no. 77*)

DÉCOUPAGE FRIEZE

This striking wall frieze was inspired by tiles at Lahore fort, in Pakistan. The design has been recreated using thin card. Lengths of card painted dark blue were used for the frieze itself, which was pasted to the red wall. The shapes were then cut out from more card, which had been painted bright blue, yellow and red. All of the paintwork was intentionally streaky, to add to the texture. Finally, the frieze was given several coats of varnish.

South Asian Designs

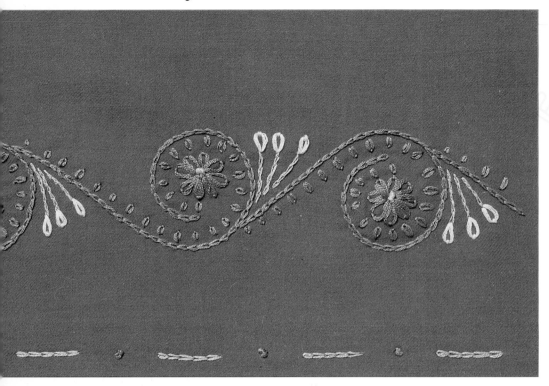

For floral-scroll border motif, see page 188 (no. 89)

EMBROIDERED WRAP

A type of Indian folk art known as 'pat' painting was the basis of the hand-embroidered decoration on this Viyella wrap. Here, it has been worked in chain stitch and detached chain stitch, also known as daisy stitch.

STENCILED TOY CHEST

These motifs were taken from a Rajasthan manuscript c. 1630, and an elephant's saddle cloth from the Deccan. One stencil was used for the elephants, another for the saddle cloths, a third for the leaves between the elephants and a fourth for the border on the top and ends. Details were hand-painted.

For elephant motif, see page 180 (no. 25)
For flower-and-leaf border motif, see page 188 (no. 94)

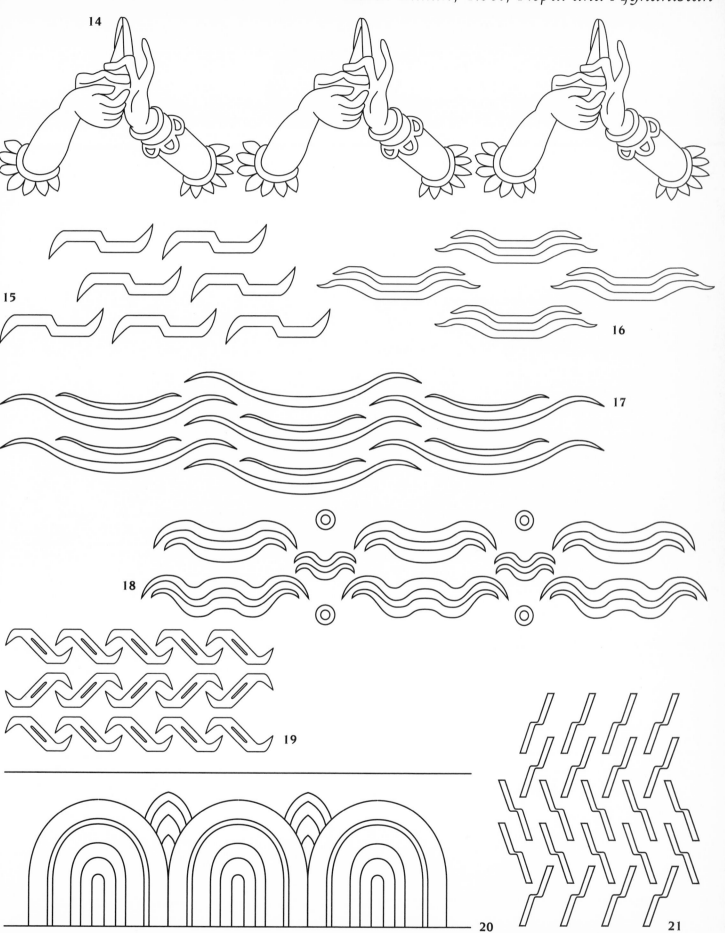

22

23

24

25

26

27

28

29

30

31

32

33

34

35

36

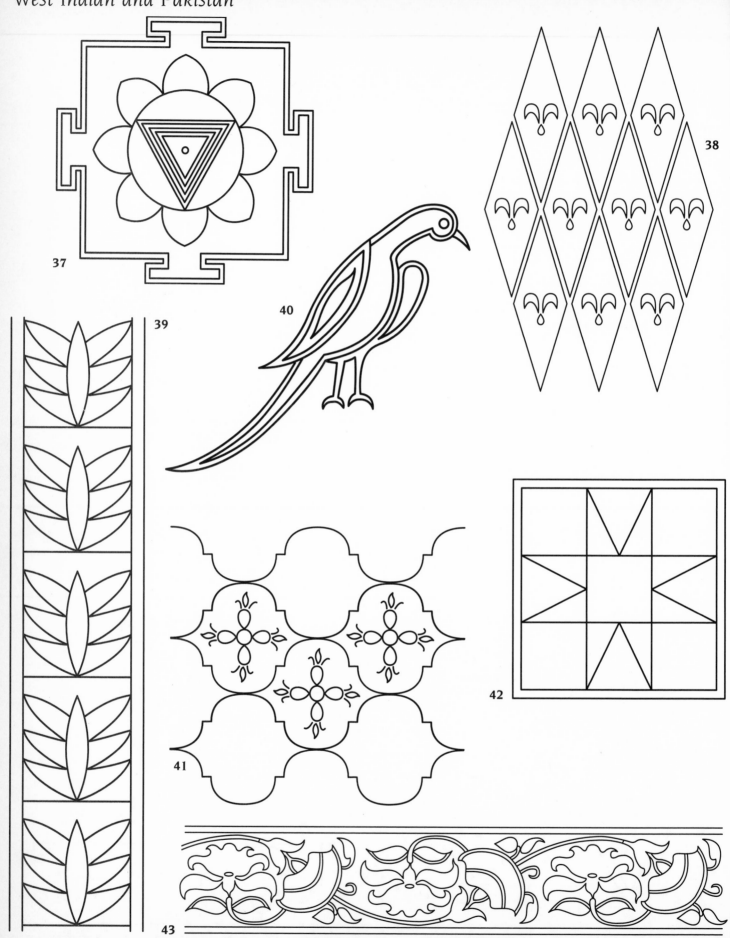

37

38

39

40

41

42

43

44

45

46

47

48

49

50

59

60

61

62

63

64

65

66

67

68

69

70

71

72

73

74

75

76

77

78

79

80

81

82

83

84

85

86

87

88

89

90

91

92

93

94

95

96

97

98

99

100

101

102

103

104

105

East Indian

106

107

108

109

110

111

112

113

114

115

NORTH AND SOUTH AMERICAN DESIGNS

Native American

1. 19th-century frieze, Woodland Indians, Great Lakes. **2.** Modern design, southern Great Lakes. **3.** Utami tribe, British Columbia. **4.** From southern Great Lakes. **5.** Ungara Indians, Hudson's Bay. **6.** Haida tribe, Canada. **7.** From Eastern Woodlands. **8.** From Eastern Woodlands. **9.** From Colorado River. **10.** Comanche blanket. **11.** From Eastern Woodlands. **12.** Yuma tribe, Colorado River. **13.** *see* 12. **14.** *see* 12. **15.** *see* 12. **16.** Border from Casas Grandes. **17.** *see* 16. **18.** Arapaho Indian shirt. **19.** Hopi Indian straw workbox. **20.** 19th-century design, Canadian Indians. **21.** Pueblo dish. **22.** *see* 21. **23.** 20th-century motif. **24.** *see* 16.

North American Folk Art

25. Rose border. **26.** New England gravestone. **27.** Pennsylvanian manuscript. **28.** Baltimore quilt. **29.** 19th-century tablecloth. **30.** Pennsylvanian chair. **31.** Quilt border. **32.** Appliqué quilt. **33.** *see* 32. **34.** 19th-century quilt design. **35.** Quilt edging. **36.** *see* 34. **37.** Wall, Pennsylvanian barn. **38.** New England weathervane. **39.** Pennsylvanian quilt. **40.** *see* 37. **41.** 19th-century Jacquard coverlet. **42.** 19th-century Pennsylvanian drawing. **43.** *see* 37. **44.** 18th-century gravestone carving. **45.** *see* 44. **46.** *see* 44. **47.** *see* 44. **48.** *see* 39. **49.** Primitive painting. **50.** 19th-century tablecloth. **51.** *see* 41. **52.** 19th-century Arabic lattice pattern. **53.** 19th-century quilt. **54.** *see* 39. **55.** 19th-century 'sawtooth' design. **56.** *see* 39.

American Art Deco

57. Metalwork door. **58.** Modern abstract design. **59.** Art Deco metalwork door. **60.** *see* 59. **61.** *see* 58. **62.** *see* 59. **63.** *see* 58. **64.** *see* 58.

Central and South American

65. Guatemalan blouse. **66.** Pre-Columbian pottery urn. **67.** Guatemalan embroidered short trousers. **68.** Bolivian hatband. **69.** Panamanian waistcoat. **70.** *see* 68. **71.** Guatemalan weaving. **72.** Woman's waistband. **73.** Man's headcloth. **74.** Guatemalan embroidery. **75.** *see* 72. **76.** *see* 74. **77.** Man's velvet overpants. **78.** Guatemalan shoulder blanket. **79.** Mexican blouse. **80.** Huichol shoulder bag. **81.** Mexican woven pattern. **82.** Shoulder bag. **83.** *see* 79. **84.** Mexican tunic. **85.** *see* 80. **86.** *see* 81. **87.** *see* 80. **88.** Mexican women's collars and cuffs. **89.** *see* 81. **90.** 15–16th-century design from an Inca jar. **91.** Inca cotton overshirt. **92.** *see* 90. **93.** 7–10th-century symbolic devices. **94.** Peruvian snakes. **95.** 11–16th-century woven border. **96.** Inca bowl. **97.** 14–16th-century woven design. **98.** 6–8th-century pottery design. **99.** Peruvian woven design. **100.** Woven textile design from pre-Columbian Peru. **101.** 12–7th-century BC design. **102.** Peruvian pre-Columbian textile design. **103.** 11–15th-century Peruvian woven motif. **104.** Peruvian woven cloth. **105.** Peruvian 11–14th-century pattern.

ANCIENT GREEK AND ROMAN DESIGNS

Minoan and Etruscan

1. Theran frieze. **2.** Theran Fresco. **3.** Mural from palace at Knossos. **4.** Wall painting, Tarquinia, Italy. **5.** *see* 4. **6.** Seal impression from Lerna. **7.** Bronze container. **8.** Theran pottery jar. **9.** Theran ewer. **10.** Pottery jug. **11.** *see* 2. **12.** Bronze mirror. **13.** Terracotta chest. **14.** *see* 13. **15.** *see* 7. **16.** Cretan tankard. **17.** Amphora. **18.** Fresco. **19.** *see* 18. **20.** *see* 7. **21.** 2nd-century BC jar. **22.** Wall of throne room in Knossos. **23.** *see* 7.

Ancient Greek

24. Urns, amphorae and vases. **25.** *see* 24. **26.** *see* 24. **27.** Plate. **28.** Border pattern. **29.** Pottery cup. **30.** Vase pattern. **31.** Athenian dish. **32.** Variation of key pattern. **33.** *see* 31. **34.** *see* 31. **35.** *see* 28. **36.** Vases, plates and pottery. **37.** Pottery design. **38.** Based on spiral from amphora from Melos. **39.** *see* 37. **40.** *see* 24. **41.** Neck of amphora. **42.** Cup. **43.** *see* 36. **44.** From a vase. **45.** *see* 31. **46.** *see* 32. **47.** *see* 31. **48.** *see* 30. **49.** *see* 38. **50.** Mosaic from Corinth. **51.** Border design. **52.** *see* 32. **53.** *see* 36. **54.** Shield. **55.** *see* 51. **56.** *see* 31. **57.** Amphora from Melos. **58.** *see* 54. **59.** Nessos amphora. **60.** *see* 57. **61.** *see* 38. **62.** *see* 36. **63.** *see* 36. **64.** *see* 32. **65.** *see* 38. **66.** *see* 31.

Ancient Roman

67. Pompeiian wall painting. **68.** Wreaths and garlands. **69.** Olive frieze. **70.** Patterns from Imperial villa, Boscotrecase. **71.** *see* 67. **72.** Acanthus leaf frieze. **73.** Pompeiian wall. **74.** Mosaic in Herculaneum. **75.** Gladiator's shield. **76.** Pompeiian mural in 'The House of Venus'. **77.** Leaf border. **78.** Roman rosette. **79.** Mosaic frieze. **80.** Pompeiian room. **81.** Borders and moldings. **82.** *see* 78. **83.** Stucco decoration. **84.** *see* 78. **85.** *see* 73. **86.** Architectural design. **87.** Architectural border. **88.** Architectural rosette. **89.** *see* 88. **90.** *see* 88. **91.** *see* 88. **92.** *see* 88. **93.** *see* 83. **94.** Pompeiian panel. **95.** *see* 81. **96.** *see* 88. **97.** Frieze, Boscoreale. **98.** Door, Boscoreale. **99.** *see* 68. **100.** *see* 68. **101.** *see* 81. **102.** *see* 78. **103.** *see* 88. **104.** *see* 78. **105.** *see* 70. **106.** Stucco palm. **107.** Architectural design. **108.** *see* 81. **109.** Leaves and berries. **110.** Painted vaulted ceiling. **111.** Square panel. **112.** *see* 68. **113.** *see* 68. **114.** *see* 78. **115.** *see* 78.

EGYPTIAN AND AFRICAN DESIGNS

Ancient Egyptian

1. Box from Tutankhamen's tomb. **2.** Cosmetic spoon. **3.** From burial chamber of king of Thebes. **4.** From Tutankhamen's tomb. **5.** Limestone relief. **6.** Pottery bowl. **7.** Lily frieze. **8.** Scarab. **9.** Symbol of SMA meaning 'union'. **10.** Papyrus painting. **11.** *see* 4. **12.** *see* 8. **13.** *see* 4. **14.** *see* 10. **15.** *see* 10. **16.** Petal design. **17.** The Udjat or Sacred Eye to ward off bad luck. **18.** *see* 6. **19.** Painted ceiling. **20.** Sign of ANKH meaning 'life'. **21.** *see* 8. **22.** *see* 10. **23.** *see* 4. **24.** From tomb of Sobkhotpe. **25.** Model of Asian adversary of Egypt. **26.** Painted manuscript. **27.** Seal. **28.** Queen Nefertiti's necklace. **29.** *see* 10. **30.** Seal.

North African

31. Mosaic or 'zillij' from house, Morocco. **32.** Wall in Ouloumbini, Mauritania. **33.** Malian cloth. **34.** Painted wall pattern. **35.** Design incised into Djenne figure. **36.** From Berber tent. **37.** 'Bogolan' or mud cloth, Mali. **38.** Door. **39.** Knotted rug, Morocco. **40.** Tiled pattern called 'Darj W Ktaf' from mosque, Fez, Morocco. **41.** Moroccan rug. **42.** Frame of door, Mauritania. **43.** Wall design. **44.** Arabic-influenced relief, Oualata, Mauritania. **45.** Fulani blanket, Mali. **46.** Wall. **47.** Interior wall painting from Soninke people, Ouloumbini, Mauritania. **48.** *see* 33. **49.** Fulami tribe, Mali. **50.** Frieze. **51.** Relief plasterwork from Mauritania called 'Mother of Thighs'. **52.** *see* 42. **53.** Inside wall. **54.** Wall from Soninke family home, Mauritania. **55.** 'Zillij' or mosaic pattern.

Central and East African

56. Ceiling of Debre Berhan Selassie. **57.** Body decoration from Surma tribesman. **58.** Loin cloth, Zaire. **59.** Ethiopian motif. **60.** *see* 58. **61.** Carved window, Bete Mikael church, Ethiopia. **62.** Lalibela cross from church, Lalibela village, Ethiopia. **63.** By Tutsi women, Rwanda. **64.** Body decoration from Surma tribesman. **65.** *see* 60. **66.** Woven skirt, Kuba, Zaire. **67.** Lid of Tutsi basket, Rwanda. **68.** Carved window, Bete Mariam church, Ethiopia. **69.** Falasha star of David, village church, Ethiopia. **70.** From L'Uélé region, Zaire. **71.** 'Agakoko', basket-work tray, Rwanda.

South African

72. Earthenware pot, Kwazulu, Natal. **73.** Zulu snuff container. **74.** By Masarna people, Botswana. **75.** San tribe, Windhoek, Namibia. **76.** Made with glass beadwork on white ground, Ndebele. **77.** Engraved ostrich egg, San tribe. **78.** *see* 77. **79.** Wood carving on Shona headrest, Zimbabwe. **80.** Ndebele beadwork. **81.** Zulu earplugs. **82.** Ndebele sheepskin coat. **83.** *see* 81. **84.** *see* 81. **85.** *see* 80.

West African

86. Exterior wall of mud hut, Burkino Faso. **87.** Cotton cloth, Kpandu, Ghana. **88.** Ashanti block print, Ghana. **89.** Wood block print, Ghana. **90.** Asafo flag, Ghana. **91.** Cloth from Korhogo, Ivory Coast. **92.** Interior wall. **93.** 1970s cotton kanga. **94.** Ghanian weaving. **95.** *see* 91. **96.** Nigerian man's robe. **97.** Yoruba tribe, Nigeria. **98.** *see* 96. **99.** Chicks circling a bowl of water. **100.** *see* 94. **101.** Ghanian flag. **102.** *see* 90. **103.** *see* 90. **104.** Modern textile print, Akosombo, Ghana. **105.** Woven cotton cloth. **106.** Wall of village shrine, Abatete, Nigeria. **107.** *see* 90. **108.** Modern textile design known as 'Hands and fingers', the Ivory Coast. **109.** *see* 90. **110.** *see* 90. **111.** *see* 104. **112.** *see* 91.

ORIENTAL DESIGNS

Chinese

1. Porcelain. **2.** Silk pillow, Western Han. **3.** Ming dynasty jar. **4.** China bottle. **5.** Dress of 17th-century Famille Vert figure made in China for export to West. **6.** Yin/Yang sign. **7.** *see* 4. **8.** Enamelled bottle. **9.** 2nd-century BC pattern from the Han dynasty. **10.** Cloisonné vase. **11.** Silk damask, Northern Dynasties. **12.** Fu-dog from Ningxia carpet. **13.** Enamelled bottles and blue and white china. **14.** *see* 4 **15.** Painted china bottle. **16.** Woven silk from Tang dynasty probably for export to West. **17.** Bronze dish. **18.** *see* 17. **19.** Design from Northern Dynasties. **20.** Enamelled vase. **21.** Painted vase. **22.** Silk embroidery. **23.** *see* 4. **24.** 17th-century Famille Vert tureen. **25.** China and enamelware. **26.** Endless knot. **27.** Dish, Hsiiag Te period. **28.** Kesi table, late Ming dynasty. **29.** Woven silk. **30.** Pwa-Kua, used in feng shui with trigrams from the I Ching. **31.** Pottery bowl. **32.** Embroidered dragon banner.

Japanese

33. Stylized design. **34.** 18th-century kimono. **35.** 17–18th-century Noh costume. **36.** Textile design. **37.** Maple leaf. **38.** Dragonfly. **39.** Gourd, kimono fabric. **40.** Persimmon, kimono. **41.** *see* 39. **42.** Plant, kimono. **43.** From old book of patterns. **44.** *see* 43. **45.** Circle of fans. **46.** *see* 39. **47.** Circular columbine pattern. **48.** Arita-ware dish, Kanei period (1624–1643). **49.** *see* 48. **50.** *see* 43. **51.** Circular wisteria. **52.** Noh costume. **53.** Flower. **54.** 19th-century enamel case. **55.** *see* 36. **56.** Bamboo, kimono fabric. **57.** *see* 43. **58.** Fabric design. **59.** *see* 47. **60.** *see* 51. **61.** Paulownia leaf, bronze plate. **62.** *see* 36. **63.** *see* 42.

Korean

64. 18–19th-century lacquer table. **65.** Printed pojagi (wrapping cloth). **66.** Pen-and-ink painting, Yi dynasty. **67.** Iron helmet. **68.** *see* 64. **69.** Peony (the symbol of longevity) pattern from Tangch'aebos, for wrapping wedding boxes. **70.** *see* 69. **71.** Kumbakpo, printed silk wrapping cloth for wedding gifts. **72.** Celadon glazed plate. **73.** Ribbon to tie up wedding boxes. **74.** *see* 72. **75.** Hemp pojagi (wrapping cloth) called a Tangch'aebo, for wrapping wedding boxes. **76.** Pojagi (wrapping cloth). **77.** Iron helmet made by Choson dynasty. **78.** Design cut out from paper and stuck onto shikjibo (pojagi made from oiled paper for covering food). **79.** *see* 76. **80.** *see* 78. **81.** Lacquer box. **82.** *see* 76. **83.** Celadon glazed dish, Koryo dynasty. **84.** *see* 77. **85.** *see* 83. **86.** Lacquer box, Choson dynasty. **87.** *see* 72.

Indonesian

88. Batik tablecloth. **89.** 'Isen' pattern. **90.** Woven cloth, Sumatra. **91.** *see* 90. **92.** Cotton karin (waistcoat), north coast of Java. **93.** Sarong. **94.** Tumbal design from silk sarong, Bali. A tumbal (triangular) design is a symbol of fertility. **95.** Batik, Sumatra. **96.** Kawung pattern from royal court of Java. **97.** *see* 94. **98.** Sarong, north coast of Java. **99.** *see* 90. **100.** *see* 92. **101.** Batik karin (waistcoat), Java. **102.** *see* 93. **103.** Sash or breast cloth. **104.** Batik kawung pattern from sarong. **105.** Batik table runner. **106.** *see* 98. **107.** Batik border design called 'cimukirran'. **108.** Early batik design using rice instead of wax. **109.** *see* 107. **110.** *see* 93. **111.** Painted cloth from Bali. **112.** *see* 111. **113.** 'Banji' symbol, meaning happiness, longevity, wealth. **114.** Painted cloth from Bali, used to separate scenes in Hindu myths.

MEDITERRANEAN DESIGNS

French

1. Provençal pattern. **2.** Henri Matisse (1953). **3.** Ring design by Francis Jourdain for Aubusson (1932). **4.** 'The Spray' by Henri Matisse (1953). **5.** Empire damask pattern. **6.** 17th-century woven silk bedcover. **7.** 18–19th-century toile de Jouy designs. **8.** 18th-century bedhanging. **9.** Geometric design, Oberkampf factory. **10.** *see* 6. **11.** Pottery bowl. **12.** *see* 9. **13.** Rim of 18th-century plate. **14.** Border of hearts from 'The Thousand and One Nights', Henri Matisse (1950). **15.** 19th-century border from bedhangings. **16.** Empire-style brocade design. **17.** *see* 9. **18.** *see* 6. **19.** *see* 7. **20.** 19th-century seat covers and hangings. **21.** *see* 20. **22.** Empire chair cover. **23.** Provençal pattern. **24.** 19th-century border, Alsace. **25.** 18th-century pottery plate. **26.** *see* 23. **27.** Cotton toile de Jouy border. **28.** *see* 8. **29.** Embroidery on bolero for Elsa Schiaparelli's 'Circus Collection', 1938. **30.** Provençal design showing Roman roots. **31.** Napoleonic bee. **32.** Provençal medallion. **33.** 1940 embroidery design by Lesage used on waistcoat by Elsa Schiaparelli. **34.** *see* 33. **35.** *see* 20. **36.** 19th-century Savoie border from pottery dish. **37.** Fabric design by Sonia Delauney. **38.** Provençal print. **39.** By Elsa Schiaparelli for Joan Crawford in 1931. **40.** *see* 9. **41.** 1920s dress fabric design by Sonia Delauney. **42.** *see* 9. **43.** *see* 41.

Italian

44. Pottery bowl. **45.** 15th-century painting by Giovanni di Paolo from Sienna. **46.** 15th-century Venetian desk. **47.** 14th-century dress of Madonna. **48.** Inlaid panel, Sienna. **49.** Stone carving, doorway. **50.** 15th-century frieze, Florence. **51.** 14th-century medallion. **52.** 16th-century curtains, Milan. **53.** 15th-century columns, Florence. **54.** Painting of the Virgin and Child by Margarito of Arezzo in 1262. **55.** 16th-century organ, Sienna. **56.** 16th-century fresco from Palazzo Orlandini in Florence. **57.** 18th-century pottery jug. **58.** Jacket by Gianni Versace. **59.** 16th-century curtain fabric, Naples. **60.** *see* 58. **61.** 16th-century border from child's bed. **62.** *see* 55. **63.** 16th-century silk damask fabric. **64.** Dress of terracotta statue of Virgin Mary.

Motif sources

65. 15th-century bed hanging. **66.** 18th–19th-century plate. **67.** Catsuit by Gianni Versace. **68.** Painting by Margarito of Arezzo in 1262. **69.** 14th-century wall painting, castle in Piedmont. **70.** 12th-century woven cloth, Sicily. **71.** 14th-century bed. **72.** Wall decoration, 15th-century Renaissance house. **73.** 1980s design for furnishing fabrics. **74.** *see* 73. **75.** 16th-century cornice border, Renaissance house. **76.** 15th-century wall decoration, Renaissance house. **77.** *see* 73. **78.** *see* 76.

Spanish and Portuguese

79. Wall in Évora, Portugal. **80.** Dress of the Virgin from 14th-century Spanish painting. **81.** Shawl, Seville, Spain. **82.** Sleeves of toreador's suit of lights. **83.** 11th-century Spanish mural. **84.** *see* 82. **85.** Moorish tile, Alhambra Palace, Granada, Spain. **86.** Spanish lace. **87.** 16th-century Portuguese painted door. **88.** Portuguese fishing boat. **89.** *see* 88. **90.** Toreador's trousers. **91.** Spanish pottery dish. **92.** 12th-century statue of the Virgin and Child, Catalonia. **93.** *see* 87. **94.** 11th-century church, Alta Ribagorça, Spain. **95.** 14th-century siren on wooden board. **96.** Drawn by Josef Maria Jujol, Spanish architect. **97.** *see* 96. **98.** 1948 hinge made from old farm tools for Guell chapel, Spain. **99.** 19th-century chapel painting, Évora, Portugal. **100.** *see* 98. **101.** Spanish gate. **102.** *see* 96. **103.** Catalan church, Spain. **104.** 14th-century roof beams, Barcelona. **105.** Portuguese dish. **106.** 16th-century Portuguese border. **107.** 12th-century border from Spanish altar. **108.** 12th-century stone carving, Toledo. **109.** Floor tile, Vallmoll, Spain. **110.** *see* 85. **111.** Embroidery design, Salamanca, Spain. **112.** Tile, Alhambra Palace, Spain. **113.** 14th-century Spanish cupboard door. **114.** 18th-century plate, Seville, Spain. **115.** Portuguese 19th-century stained-glass window. **116.** *see* 110. **117.** *see* 110.

SCANDINAVIAN DESIGNS

Viking

1. Swedish silver bowl. **2.** Danish inlaid iron axe. **3.** Norwegian weather vane. **4.** Stone carving, Isle of Man. **5.** Danish bronze horse. **6.** Swedish rune stone design. **7.** Caedmon manuscript. **8.** Stone carving, Yorkshire. **9.** Norwegian brooch. **10.** Iron axe, Jutland. **11.** Norwegian bedpost. **12.** Carving from Danish horse collar. **13.** Gold leaves from Brangstrub, Denmark. **14.** *see* 3. **15.** Stone carving from Sweden. **16.** Wood carving from Danish church. **17.** *see* 13. **18.** Picture stone from Sweden. **19.** *see* 18. **20.** *see* 2. **21.** Danish brooch.

Swedish

22. Fur mitten. **23.** *see* 22. **24.** Border from doorway. **25.** 19th-century leather gloves. **26.** Frieze from church. **27.** 19th-century floor pattern. **28.** Frieze from farmhouse. **29.** 1787 mural by Louis Masreliez. **30.** 19th-century velvet mitten. **31.** Wall design. **32.** 1780 commode. **33.** 18th-century house. **34.** 19th-century panels. **35.** Clock face. **36.** Stenciled floor. **37.** 15th-century Härkeberga church ceiling. **38.** Wall painting called 'Kurbit', by itinerant painters. **39.** Wall, Carl Larsson's house. **40.** *see* 39. **41.** Tile design from stove. **42.** Mural. **43.** Stencil, Härkeberga church. **44.** 19th-century stenciled border. **45.** Wall stencil from church. **46.** Härkeberga church. **47.** Carl Larsson's daughter's dress. **48.** Hand-painted border. **49.** Leather glove. **50.** *see* 49. **51.** *see* 49. **52.** *see* 43. **53.** *see* 41. **54.** Mossebo church ceiling. **55.** 'Kurbit' painting. **56.** Painted panel. **57.** 1880 panel. **58.** *see* 48. **59.** *see* 41. **60.** *see* 41. **61.** Mossebo church. **62.** 1699 carved architrave. **63.** 19th-century leather glove. **64.** Border panels. **65.** 19th-century frieze. **66.** 19th-century mirror stencil. **67.** *see* 48. **68.** *see* 37. **69.** Wallpaper from 1892 Carl Larsson watercolor. **70.** Panel from Palace of Gripsholm. **71.** *see* 41.

Danish

72. 19th-century shawl. **73.** *see* 72. **74.** 19th-century cross-stitch pictures. **75.** *see* 74. **76.** *see* 74. **77.** *see* 74. **78.** *see* 74. **79.** *see* 72. **80.** *see* 72. **81.** 19th-century velvet cap. **82.** *see* 74. **83.** *see* 72. **84.** *see* 72. **85.** *see* 72.

Finnish

86. 16th-century wall hanging. **87.** 19th-century coverlet. **88.** 1721 carpet. **89.** Chalice cover, Pöytyä church. **90.** 18th-century carpet design. **91.** Woven blanket. **92.** 17th-century towel. **93.** *see* 92.

Norwegian

94. 18th-century calendar board. **95.** 5–6th-century carving. **96.** 18th-century cushion. **97.** Wood carving, bishop's chair from church, Tyldal. **98.** Woven rug. **99.** 17–18th-century incised wood. **100.** *see* 99. **101.** 17th-century carpet. **102.** Wooden butter dish. **103.** 18th-century wooden carving. **104.** *see* 96. **105.** *see* 97. **106.** 19th-century embroidery. **107.** 19th-century chest. **108.** 19th-century cloth. **109.** Yoke of 18th-century horse's bridle. **110.** Wood carving. **111.** 18th-century plate. **112.** 18th-century glove. **113.** 18th-century cushion. **114.** 16th-century linen tablecloth.

CELTIC AND BRITISH DESIGNS

Celtic

1. Irish wirework. **2.** Trier Gospels. **3.** Enamelwork. **4.** The Book of Lindisfarne. **5.** *see* 1. **6.** 3rd-century BC helmet. **7.** *see* 4. **8.** Armlets from Perthshire. **9.** Lindisfarne Gospel c. 690. **10.** Engraved on cauldron. **11.** *see* 9. **12.** 1st-century Welsh tankard. **13.** Durham 'Cassiodorus' (illuminated Bible). **14.** Bronze disk, Ireland. **15.** Bone carving, Ireland. **16.** 'Canterbury Codex Aureus'.

Medieval

17. Effigy of Queen Eleanor, Westminster Abbey. **18.** Holkham Bible. **19.** Church window. **20.** Illuminated manuscript. **21.** Luttrell Psalter. **22.** Chasuble. **23.** 14th-century effigy. **24.** 14th-century Book of Hours. **25.** Illuminated letter. **26.** 14th-century King John cup. **27.** 15th-century rood screen. **28.** *see* 21. **29.** *see* 21. **30.** Chronicle of Peterborough Abbey. **31.** Bromholm Psalter, Norwich. **32.** *see* 27. **33.** 15th-century church window. **34.** Rood screen. **35.** *see* 33. **36.** *see* 20. **37.** Peterborough Psalter.

Elizabethan

38. Sampler. **39.** Stomacher. **40.** *see* 39. **41.** Cushion. **42.** Hood. **43.** Bedspread. **44.** *see* 39. **45.** Coif. **46.** Curtain.

Georgian and Regency

47. Staffordshire creamware jug. **48.** Basaltware teapot. **49.** *see* 47. **50.** Teapot. **51.** Staffordshire creamware teapot. **52.** *see* 47. **53.** Davenham teapot. **54.** Spitalfields silk waistcoat fabric. **55.** Spitalfields silk. **56.** *see* 55. **57.** *see* 48. **58.** *see* 54. **59.** *see* 54. **60.** Silk weaver's pattern book, 1805. **61.** *see* 60. **62.** *see* 55.

Victorian

63. Aesthetic movement. **64.** *see* 63. **65.** Tile designed by William Morris. **66.** *see* 65. **67.** *see* 63. **68.** 1885 tile by Morris, Marshall, Faulkner & Co. **69.** 1887 Holland Park carpet, William Morris. **70.** Silver Studio, 1905. **71.** *see* 70. **72.** 1863 stained-glass panel by Morris, Marshall, Faulkner & Co. **73.** Knotted design. **74.** *see* 72. **75.** *see* 63. **76.** Harry Silver. **77.** *see* 76. **78.** William Morris tapestry design. **79.** Tile by William de Morgan. **80.** *see* 65. **81.** 1870 tile by Burne-Jones. **82.** 1861 ceiling, William Morris's own Red House. **83.** 1885 dado from Silver Studio. **84.** 1899 wallpaper design, Silver Studio. **85.** *see* 83.

Art Nouveau and Art Deco

86. 1930s design, Phyllis Barron and Dorothy Larcher partnership. **87.** *see* 86. **88.** 1939 design, Old Beach Linen Co. **89.** 1930s woodblock print, Enid Marx. **90.** *see* 86. **91.** 1932 glass design, Keith Murray. **92.** 1934 design, Campbell fabrics. **93.** 1934 printed cotton crêpe. **94.** *see* 86. **95.** 1930s dress fabric. **96.** 1930s crêpe de chine fabric. **97.** 1934 block print by Mea Angerer.

Bloomsbury Group

98. 1940 mirror frame by Duncan Grant in 1940. **99.** Frieze design. **100.** 1934 soup bowl by Duncan Grant for Clarice Cliff. **101.** Mantelpiece design, Vanessa Bell. **102.** Wall stencil from Charleston. **103.** 1917 line drawing on cupboard door by Vanessa Bell. **104.** Stencil by Vanessa Bell, painted together with Duncan Grant in 1940.

NORTHERN EUROPEAN DESIGNS

German

1. Carved panel. **2.** 18th-century frieze. **3.** 19th-century basket. **4.** *see* 1. **5.** 19th-century panel. **6.** 19th-century Bavarian design. **7.** 19th-century Bavarian flower. **8.** Painted drawer. **9.** 18th-century carved panel. **10.** 19th-century cupboard. **11.** 19th-century wooden panel. **12.** Hand-painted design. **13.** Trunk border. **14.** Cupboard border. **15.** Antique trunk. **16.** 1921 Bauhaus design. **17.** 1927 Bauhaus design. **18.** *see* 16. **19.** *see* 11.

Austrian and Hungarian

20. 1905 frieze design, Gustav Klimt. **21.** 13th-century cope. **22.** *see* 21. **23.** 1911 Faïence dish. **24.** 1920 endpaper design from book, Wiener Werkstätte. **25.** 1915 fashion plate. **26.** 1914 Austrian fashion poster. **27.** 1920 Austrian pottery service. **28.** Viennese vase. **29.** *see* 21. **30.** 1910 Austrian book cover. **31.** Plate, Salzkammergut. **32.** 1918 Austrian tulle and lace cover. **33.** 1919 wine label, Wiener Werkstätte. **34.** Hungarian hemp design. **35.** Hungarian towel. **36.** *see* 35. **37.** Hungarian inlaid panel. **38.** Hungarian pillow slip. **39.** Hungarian salt cellar. **40.** Hungarian bridal chest. **41.** *see* 39. **42.** Hungarian funeral sheet. **43.** Hungarian ceiling, Calvinist church. **44.** *see* 39. **45.** *see* 42. **46.** 19th-century Hungarian plate. **47.** *see* 46. **48.** *see* 43.

Czech

49. Dish. **50.** Belt. **51.** 19th-century pitcher. **52.** Chest. **53.** Easter egg. **54.** *see* 53. **55.** Block print. **56.** Woodblock fabric. **57.** Marquetry design. **58.** Biscuit mold. **59.** Painted cupboard. **60.** *see* 53. **61.** *see* 55. **62.** Leather belt.

Polish

63. Ribbon, 16th-century cope. **64.** 17th-century brocade. **65.** Terracotta tile. **66.** 17th-century sword cover. **67.** 17th-century sword hilt. **68.** 19th-century plate. **69.** *see* 67. **70.** *see* 68. **71.** *see* 65. **72.** *see* 68. **73.** *see* 65. **74.** Jug. **75.** Leaf pattern. **76.** Single leaf. **77.** Ribbon, 18th-century cope. **78.** *see* 68.

Rumanian

79. Tile. **80.** Design on glass. **81.** 18th-century tile. **82.** 18th-century stone carving. **83.** 18th-century tile. **84.** Tile. **85.** Painting of 'The Last Supper'. **86.** *see* 85. **87.** Religious painting. **88.** Painting of the Madonna. **89.** Glass painting. **90.** *see* 89. **91.** Harlequin pattern from bench. **92.** *see* 87. **93.** *see* 85. **94.** Water pattern.

Russian

95. 19th-century design. **96.** 19th-century motifs. **97.** Lacquer box. **98.** 1928 teaplate. **99.** *see* 96. **100.** Woman's dress. **101.** *see* 100. **102.** Side of a revolutionary propaganda train in 1919. **103.** Painted box design. **104.** 19th-century leaf. **105.** 1923 teaplate by Tchekhonin. **106.** Frieze. **107.** 1930s textile design. **108.** 1925 china plate. **109.** *see* 108. **110.** *see* 108. **111.** 1920s textile design. **112.** 18th-century towel.

SOUTH ASIAN DESIGNS

North Indian, Tibet, Nepal and Afghanistan

1. Afghan saddlebag. **2.** Beam, Ladakh, Kashmir. **3.** Silk bag. **4.** Tile. **5.** Miniature painting. **6.** 18th-century sari miniature. **7.** Rug design meaning 'forty rams'. **8.** *see* 1. **9.** *see* 1. **10.** Block print, Punjab. **11.** Floor painting, Himachal Pradesh. **12.** Turkoman Bukhara rug. **13.** Turkoman rug design meaning 'camel teeth'. **14.** 18th-century painting from Nepal. **15.** Tibetan Tiger rug. **16.** *see* 15. **17.** *see* 15. **18.** *see* 15. **19.** *see* 15 **20.** *see* 2. **21.** *see* 15.

West Indian and Pakistan

22. Canvas pavilion. **23.** Silver necklace, Gujarat. **24.** 19th-century block print, Rajasthan. **25.** 17th-century Samgrahanisutra manuscript, Rajasthan. **26.** 17th-century temple hanging, Rajasthan. **27.** 18th-century brooch. **28.** Block print, Rajasthan turban. **29.** 18th-century Rajasthan painting. **30.** 16th-century Kalpasutra manuscript. **31.** *see* 30. **32.** *see* 30. **33.** 19th-century brooch. **34.** 18th–19th-century embroidery, Gujarat. **35.** Gujarat embroidery . **36.** Block print, Gujarat. **37.** 'Kali Yantra' 18th-century religious painting, Gujarat. **38.** Woven cloth, Pakistan. **39.** 15th-century border, Gujarat. **40.** 19th-century textile design, Gujarat. **41.** 18th-century balustrade, Gujarat. **42.** 20th-century design, Gujarat. **43.** *see* 36. **44.** Tile mosaic, fort in Lahore, Pakistan. **45.** Embroidered shawl. **46.** *see* 41. **47.** 18th-century miniature of a Maharaja's coat, Rajasthan. **48.** *see* 28. **49.** 19th-century fabric. **50.** *see* 44. **51.** Temple hanging, Gujarat. **52.** *see* 44. **53.** *see* 45. **54.** *see* 28. **55.** *see* 40. **56.** *see* 28. **57.** *see* 44. **58.** 17th-century Upadesamala manuscript. **59.** *see* 40. **60.** *see* 44. **61.** *see* 40. **62.** 17th-century mystical diagram, Gujarat. **63.** *see* 44. **64.** *see* 28. **65.** *see* 44.

Central and South Indian

66. Deccan elephant's saddlecloth. **67.** 19th-century block print. **68.** 17th-century Bidri ewer from the Deccan. **69.** 17th-century Bidri tray from the Deccan. **70.** Festival floor painting, Andhra Pradesh. **71.** *see* 69. **72.** Floor painting from Tamil Nadu. **73.** Woven shawl border. **74.** *see* 72. **75.** 18th-century shrine in the Deccan. **76.** 19th-century block print from Madhya Pradesh. **77.** Camel saddle cover, Hyderabad. **78.** *see* 68. **79.** Carpet border from miniature. **80.** 19th-century cotton hanging, southern India. **81.** Sash from a miniature. **82.** *see* 70. **83.** Textile design from Karnataka. **84.** *see* 66. **85.** 17th-century Mughal miniature. **86.** *see* 69.

East Indian

87. Woven head covering, Uttar Pradesh. **88.** *see* 87. **89.** Pat-painting, Puri. **90.** Sandstone archway, Uttar Pradesh. **91.** Block print. **92.** Woven pattern, Uttar Pradesh. **93.** *see* 92. **94.** Saddlecloth. **95.** Floor painting, Uttar Pradesh. **96.** Painting, Bihar. **97.** Embroidered waistcoat. **98.** 19th-century woven design, Uttar Pradesh. **99.** 15th-century Jain manuscript, Uttar Pradesh. **100.** Carved stone medallion, Uttar Pradesh. **101.** 19th-century embroidery, Uttar Pradesh. **102.** *see* 100. **103.** *see* 100. **104.** *see* 90. **105.** Geometric motif called 'Buti'. **106.** Design, Uttar Pradesh. **107.** *see* 99. **108.** *see* 99. **109.** *see* 99. **110.** *see* 99. **111.** *see* 101. **112.** *see* 90. **113.** Vase, Uttar Pradesh. **114.** *see* 89. **115.** *see* 100.